Sovereign Risk Analysis

Sovereign Risk Analysis

Shelagh A. Heffernan

The City University Business School, London

London
ALLEN & UNWIN
Boston   Sydney

Allen & Unwin (Publishers) Ltd,
40 Museum Street, London WC1A 1LU, UK

Allen & Unwin (Publishers) Ltd,
Park Lane, Hemel Hempstead, Herts HP2 4TE, UK

Allen & Unwin Inc.,
8 Winchester Place, Winchester, Mass 01890, USA

Allen & Unwin (Australia) Ltd,
8 Napier Street, North Sydney, NSW 2060, Australia

First published in 1986

British Library Cataloguing in Publication Data

Heffernan, Shelagh A.
    Sovereign risk analysis.
1. Debts, External   2. Debts, Public
3. Risk
I. Title
336.3'6   HJ8015
ISBN 0–04–332119–4

Library of Congress Cataloging in Publication Data

Heffernan, Shelagh A., 1956–
    Sovereign risk analysis.
Bibliography: p.
Includes index.
1. Loans, Foreign—Evaluation.   2. Risk.
3. Debts, External. I. Title.
HG3891.5.H44   1986   332.1'5'0685   85–32069
ISBN 0–04–332119–4 (alk. paper)

Set in 10 on 11 point Imprint by Bedford Typesetters Ltd, Bedford, and printed in Great Britain by Billings, Worcester

Contents

Acknowledgements

I am indebted to a number of colleagues who provided helpful comments on different chapters in this book. In particular I would like to thank Michael Beenstock, Alfred Kenyon and Richard Taffler. I am also grateful for the contributions made by MBA students who took the MBA elective on Country Risk Analysis, held at CUBS each summer term. Two referees also provided useful suggestions and pointed out some important omissions. Finally, I would like to give a special acknowledgement to Peter Sinclair, who raises the intellectual standard of our home life to a level well above that of any seminar in international finance.

To the Staff and Students at CUBS, 1982–5

Introduction

The subject of this book is the analysis of sovereign risk. The purpose of sovereign risk analysis (SRA) is to identify those cases where countries are unable to meet their commitments on their sovereign external debt. A nation's external debt consists of loans made by non-residents, repayable in foreign currency, goods and services. The debt may be short term, medium term, or long term with associated maturities of less than one year, up to seven years, and more than seven years respectively. When a country originally incurs external debt through the disbursement of a foreign loan, this debt appears as an inflow on the capital account of the balance of payments. Repayment of the principal is registered as a capital outflow, whereas payment of interest adds to the deficit or subtracts from the surplus of the current account. This distinguishes a loan negotiated on international markets from a domestic loan, which has no influence on the country's balance of payments.

However, in common with any loan, there is a critical time-element attached to foreign loans. The lender agrees to disburse the loan at one point of time, to be repaid at a later date. The lender can only assess the riskiness of the loan based on ex ante information about the borrower. The risk assumed by the lender is the ability of the borrower to repay the loan at the time specified.

External debt can be placed in one of two classifications. First, there is the category of *sovereign* external debt: this consists of all publicly guaranteed loans granted to a foreign firm by a private bank or loans made directly to a foreign government. Secondly, there is non publicly guaranteed *private* external debt. This debt consists of loans granted to a foreign private individual or firm, for which the foreign government has no responsibility.

Sovereign Risk Analysis concerns itself with an analysis of the risks associated with loans in the first category. These loans are termed sovereign loans to emphasize that the ultimate responsibility for repayment rests with a government. A bank can agree to grant a sovereign loan to the government of its own country, but this will add to the internal indebtedness of the country and have no implications for the country's balance of payments. None the less, much of the analysis in this book could also be applied to sovereign internal debt because, as will become apparent to the reader of this book, the uniqueness of the loan lies in the fact that it is a government which has the ultimate responsibility for repayment.

Loans which fall into the category of private external debt are not the subject of this book. From the standpoint of the lending bank, a non-guaranteed private loan is not very different from other loans the bank makes because the responsibility for repayment rests with an individual or firm. Should the entity default on its debt, the bank can resort to the usual remedies, including the acquisition of the defaulter's assets as compensation for the default. Therefore, the bank can employ its usual credit assessment techniques, with two qualifications. The cross border nature of the loan means the lender may be subject to political interference by the host government, especially if the 'foreign' private bank attempts to acquire assets in the event of default. Although this problem is not one which is exclusive to foreign governments, the bank is likely to know less about foreign government machinery than that of the government of the country where it has its headquarters. This increases the political uncertainty associated with cross-border private loans. An additional risk arises because of the possibility of exchange controls, which may make it difficult for an entity to repatriate borrowed foreign capital. While these qualifications do distinguish this type of loan from domestic private loans, the problems do not warrant a book devoted to their analysis. The difficulties inherent in sovereign lending do.

Sovereign risk analysis is concerned with the estimation of the probability of default on sovereign external debt. However, a problem arises from the use of the term default because the ultimate responsibility for repayment of a sovereign loan rests with a government. Hence, a lender would have to declare a country insolvent if the term default is to have its usual meaning. But it is very difficult to conceive of an insolvent nation. For example, in 1949 China repudiated its external debt obligations, but no lender could declare the country insolvent in the way it might an individual or firm. Even if it were possible to define an insolvent country, what would such a declaration imply for the lenders? These are issues that are considered more carefully in this book.

Recognizing the problems that arise if default is used in the normal sense of the word, default on a sovereign loan has been interpreted as either outright repudiation of the sovereign external debt or a re-scheduling of the debt. The second interpretation is problematic, a point taken up in Chapter 2. But, accepting these definitions for the moment, SRA is concerned with estimating the probability that these events will occur.

'Sovereign Risk Analysis' appears in the title of this book because of its explicit focus on this type of lending, as defined above. Some readers may equate this with the term 'country risk' analysis because of the tendency in the literature to use these terms interchangeably. The author herself has done this in the past. The reason for this probably stems from the confusion over the terms 'risk' and 'uncertainty'. An economist defines risk as being any event to which a measurable probability can be attached, but uncertainty is not measurable either because the 'event' is not easily defined and/or does not occur often enough to permit probabilities to be estimated. A good example of this lies in the area of political 'risk' analysis, where the definition of the event has been unsatisfactory and there are serious measurement problems associated with the political event.

Academics (including this author) have tended to equate country risk with sovereign risk because this is the only aspect of country risk analysis to which truly measurable probabilities can be attached. On the other hand, practitioners in the field of finance who use the terms risk and uncertainty interchangeably would be critical of the narrow interpretation given to it by academics. There is nothing wrong with either approach, but a problem arises because two conventions are being used. This author has chosen the term 'sovereign risk' in order to avoid confusion between the two groups. It will satisfy the academic who is used to the distinction between the two terms and the practitioner for whom the term country risk has a much broader meaning.

This text excludes the standard discussion of political risk analysis which, had it been included, would have lent justification to a title 'country risk' analysis. The standard discussion is normally concerned with the problems of political interference faced by foreign-owned firms in a given country. If a bank has branches located away from its home base, then it too may be subject to political interference by a host government. However, this is a problem for any firm with branches extending across national borders and is quite distinct from the risks associated with sovereign lending. It is a fascinating part of country risk analysis and the author is currently undertaking a major research project in this area. However, it is not a topic that fits well into a book devoted to an analysis of the unique problems which arise on sovereign lending. For readers interested in this aspect of country risk analysis, I recommend papers by Ghadar (1982), Heenan and Rummel (1978), the 'perspective' by Reid in a collection edited by R. J. Herring, *Managing International Risk* (1983), and Chapter 15 in a book by A. C. Shapiro entitled *Multinational Financial Management* (1982).

On the other hand, the political dimension is an important part of sovereign risk analysis. Decisions to borrow on international capital markets, to repudiate external debt repayments, and to undertake certain economic programmes will be derivatives of the political process in the borrowing country. However, the role played by political factors is quite different from that considered in the standard works on political risk (in which the authors put emphasis on political interference in foreign direct investments). Hence, the introduction of political factors in sovereign risk analysis will require an approach which is distinct from that normally seen in the political risk literature. As the reader will come to see, the political dimension forms an integral part of the broader framework for sovereign risk analysis developed in this book.

The book is organized as follows. Chapter 1 begins by exploring the broad economic reasons behind a country's (bank's) decision to borrow (lend) on international capital markets. This is followed by an analysis of the current international debt problem and a review of historical precedents. The emphasis is on the importance of random economic shocks and domestic economic policies in explaining much of the current problem. These are points that have tended to be underemphasized in the literature, to the disadvantage of students and practitioners in this field.

Chapter 2 consists of a comprehensive review of the standard approaches to sovereign risk analysis. This includes the approaches taken by the popular financial journals, *Institutional Investor* and *Euromoney*, but the statistical models receive the greatest attention. The objective in this part of the chapter is to explain the details of these models in a way that makes them accessible to individuals with no specific training in either economics or statistics. This is a very important exercise because there are many banks who either directly or indirectly use these models. However, the technical nature of the academic papers where the models are explained makes them inaccessible to all but those with a strong technical background in economics and statistics. Yet students of international finance and individuals active in the area of sovereign risk assessment need to understand the workings of the models and, more important, their deficiencies. All too often these models are blindly accepted for use by practitioners because of their apparent sophistication. This author will provide the reader with a critical analysis of these models, hoping to persuade readers that, although these models have something to offer to the sovereign risk analyst, the weight placed on their importance has been too great.

Chapter 3 represents the core of this book. The ideas will be new to most readers, and an initial reaction by some will be: 'What has all this to do with sovereign risk analysis?' This is because the theme is relatively new and has not been digested by practitioners in the area. By the end of the Chapter I hope to have won over the sceptics among you. The objective of the chapter is to place the problems of sovereign risk analysis in a much broader framework than they currently occupy. To do this, the general principles behind the demand and supply of sovereign lending are developed and applied (on a case-by-case basis) to the current international debt problems. Throughout, the stress is on the implications of this approach for the practising sovereign risk analyst. Chapter 4 presents a method for writing country reports. The chapter reviews critically the typical 'spread sheet' used by country report writers, drawing on the ideas presented in the previous two chapters.

In Chapter 5, issues of international financial stability are examined. The chapter begins by defining the meaning of terms such as financial crisis, instability, insolvency and illiquidity, and applies them to current international financial problems. This is followed by a review of the various proposals put forward to deal with the international debt problem, ranging from the non-interventionist option advocated by some policy-makers to the proposal for an international lender of last resort. Issues arising from the principal agent problem (characterized by moral hazard and the tendency to free ride) and asymmetric information are also discussed. The objective of the chapter is to answer the question: What is the optimal method of dealing with the international sovereign debt problem given the unique nature of sovereign lending and borrowing? Some readers may be of the opinion that, because the chapter does not directly address the issue of *how* sovereign risk is to be analysed, it is not important to them. This is the very attitude the book is trying to discourage. The sovereign debt problem is a global problem because it threatens the stability of the international financial system. Analysts have tended to focus on the narrow issues of this problem as it affected their banks. However, it is important for them to see the problem in a much broader perspective. Not only should this improve the decision-making process within individual banks, but it will also provide lenders with a theme that they can use to influence the policy-makers in this field.

1 A Review of the Current Situation

Introduction and Definition of Sovereign Risk Analysis

Sovereign risk analysis concerns itself with the identification of countries which will be unable to meet their commitments on sovereign external debt, defined as all cross-border loans granted by a private bank in one country directly to a foreign government or publicly guaranteed loans made to a foreign firm. Necessary prerequisites to a study of this subject are an examination of the determinants of sovereign borrowing and lending and a review of the current international debt problems. These are the objectives of this chapter. First, we analyse the economic determinants of capital flows between countries. Sovereign borrowing and lending represents one type of international capital flow. Secondly, we review the current situation (see p. 9) followed by reference to historical precedents (p. 23); a thorough examination of these two subjects establishes the framework for the forthcoming chapters.

The Economic Determinants of International Capital Flows

Prior to any review of the current international debt problem or discussion of how to analyse sovereign risk, it is necessary to examine the reasons for international capital flows, especially those that are in the form of sovereign loans. Like any economic phenomenon the question is best answered by identifying the economic determinants of these flows. For the sovereign risk analyst the exercise will be useful because it places the sovereign debt problems in a more general framework than is normally the case.

Basic principles of economics explain why cross-border lending has become an integral part of the international economy. Begin by dividing the world into two groups of economies, the 'First' World and the 'Third' World. The First World economies have a supply of capital that exceeds their domestic requirements. These are 'surplus' capital countries, often with well-developed capital markets that can provide capital at lower cost than elsewhere in the world. The theory of comparative advantage explains why the First World will want to export this capital. A country has a comparative advantage in the production of goods or services if it makes the goods or provides the services more efficiently than the rest of the world. The potential economic welfare of a country will improve if it exports goods in which it has a comparative advantage, and imports goods and services from countries that are relatively more efficient in their production. Capital is normally considered to be a factor input in the production process, but this does not exclude us from applying the principle of comparative advantage to the international trade of capital. Just as resource-rich countries export their raw materials, so efficient producers of capital will export capital. The First World consists of those countries which are efficient producers of capital and, therefore, exploit their comparative advantage by exporting the surplus capital. Third World countries are net importers of capital because their own capital base is not sufficiently well developed to meet their domestic demand requirements. The rate of return will differ in the two worlds: it will be relatively lower in the capital-abundant First World and relatively higher in the capital-deficient Third World. Trade in capital between the two groups gives rise to international flows of capital until the rates of return on capital in the two groups are equalized.

Most students of international finance will readily acknowledge that Western economic development during the past century has been responsible for the rapid expansion of the West's capital base, which in turn has created a supply of capital in excess of domestic capital requirements. The development of efficient capital markets in the West has made this First World the most efficient supplier of capital, and the rapid emergence of the oil-based economies, during the last decade, has added to this surplus capital base. Several oil-exporting nations found they had large and growing balance of payments surpluses. The revenue earned from oil was far in excess of what could be reinvested in the domestic economies of these countries. The remainder was deposited in the Western banking system, which could invest this capital in the international capital markets and earn the highest going rate of return for their customers. This 'recycling' of petrodollars reached its height in the mid-1970s and added considerably to the surplus capital base of the First World.

While the supply side of international capital markets is fairly straightforward, the demand side may be less clear-cut for those readers unfamiliar with theories of economic growth and development. Readers may be asking why Third World countries always demand capital in excess of their own domestic capital base. This is best explained by appealing to a 'development cycle' hypothesis of economic growth. According to this, countries demand capital based on expectations of higher future income streams. By borrowing capital, the country can finance higher domestic growth rates and, also, smooth its investment and consumption paths over time. This hypothesis of economic development is a broader concept than the Friedman (1957) permanent income hypothesis of consumption[1] which refers to household consumption patterns. The Friedman theory explains household borrowing and lending patterns in terms of the need to smooth consumption paths over time in the face of income disturbances, whereas in the development cycle hypothesis of economic growth the smoothing function is secondary to the main reason for borrowing: to finance a more rapid rate of growth (and therefore development) in the country than would be possible in the absence of borrowed capital.

If the country's domestic capital base is insufficient to meet its growth rate targets, it will borrow the capital from the international capital markets, that is, it will import capital. Provided the expected marginal productivity (i.e. the increase in the country's output brought about by a given unit increase in capital) of the domestic endowment of capital exceeds the rate of interest that the country pays for the employment of this external capital, the country will be a net importer of capital. This external capital will allow the country to develop its own industrial base and the foreign capital will be repatriated once the economy has reached a stage in development where the domestic resource base is sufficient to meet its own capital demands.

Before going any further it is necessary to be more precise about the meaning of a 'developing country' which is a net importer of capital. The International Monetary Fund (IMF)[2] divides developing nations into two groups. The first group consists of oil-exporting countries, where oil exports make up at least two-thirds of the country's total exports *and* the country exports at least 100 million barrels a year. Cline (1984) distinguishes between oil-exporting countries which are in capital surplus and those which are not. In the latter group are Algeria, Ecuador, Nigeria, Indonesia and Venezuela. By the IMF classification, all of these countries except Ecuador would be classified as oil-exporting countries. This is important to understand, because much of the work done by the IMF relates to sovereign debt problems of the second IMF group termed 'non oil developing countries' or 'non oil less developed countries' (NOLDCs). This second category of developing countries is in turn divided into four subgroups:

(1) The net oil-exporting countries: These countries are net exporters of oil, but do not meet the criteria cited above for oil-exporting developing country status. These include: Bahrain, Bolivia, People's Republic of the Congo, Ecuador, Egypt, Gabon, Malaysia, Mexico, Peru, Syrian Arab Republic, Trinidad and Tobago, Tunisia.

(2) Net oil-importing countries but major exporters of manufactures: Argentina, Brazil, Greece, Hong Kong, Israel, South Korea, Portugal, Singapore, South Africa, Yugoslavia. These countries tend to have a higher income per head than those in the other subgroups.

(3) Net oil-importing countries with low incomes: There are 43 countries in this group, characterised by a per capita GDP that did not exceed $350.00 in 1978. This includes countries such as the Sudan, Bangladesh, Chad, Ethiopia, India, Pakistan, Sri Lanka. A full listing can be found in Appendix B of the statistical tables in *World Economic Outlook* (IMF, 1983).

(4) Other net oil importers: these are middle-income oil-importing nations which, in general, rely on the export of primary commodities. Countries in this category include Ghana, Jamaica, the Cameroons, Uruguay.

It should be stressed that the IMF classification of developing countries relates to the industrial base of the country rather than to whether it is a net importer of capital. Indeed, there are some industrial countries in the IMF classification of developed nations which are net importers of capital, Ireland being a good example. The sub classifications of developing nations relate to their oil-importing/exporting status rather than to their capital import status. For the purposes of this book, which concentrates on the problems of sovereign debtor nations, the IMF classification is useful because those countries classified as 'non oil' developing countries are also net importers of capital. In addition there are the oil-exporting countries not in capital surplus, which were noted earlier (p. 3). Most of the statistics cited in the next section (see p. 9 ff.) relate to the non oil developing countries and therefore exclude some important debtor nations. Where possible, reference is made to the '25 major borrowers', four of these being major exporters of oil. The list of these countries is given in Table 1.1 (p. 11).

Up to this point, the reason why developing nations are net importers of capital has been explained, but no mention has been made of the special type of capital import, sovereign loans. The issue of why developing nations gear themselves in the way they do needs further scrutiny. Like any firm, a country which wishes to import capital has two options: it can find a bank willing to lend it the funds or external capital can be raised through equity financing. The latter is usually accomplished by permitting foreign direct investment in the country. In this case foreign capital is injected into the developing country through the establishment of foreign-owned plants. Another method of equity financing would be through the international sale of shares by a domestic firm; however, this is really a form of direct portfolio investment because it increases the proportion of foreign shareholders in the company. Therefore, a country has a 'foreign' gearing ratio analogous to the gearing ratio of a firm. It is defined as the ratio of foreign debt to foreign equity in a country. The external debt will consist of sovereign debt and private, non publicly guaranteed foreign debt. As was noted in the introduction to this book, the sovereign risk analyst is not directly concerned with the private type of debt and for most developing countries (as illustrated by the figures cited below) this has been a decreasing proportion of total external debt. The numerator of the ratio will also include concessional loans made to developing countries by agencies such as the World Bank. Again, they are not the direct concern of the sovereign risk analyst.

A study of the figures on the demand for external finance by developing countries reveals some interesting trends.[3] Before 1973, the principal source of external finance for developing countries was foreign direct investment. During the 1960s, it made up (on average) 39 per cent of the total of external finance for developing countries. The proportion of official finance and commercial bank loans was approximately 30 per cent for each. Between 1974 and 1983, the stock of long-term private external loans to NOLDCs increased at an annual average rate of 25.5 per cent compared with an average annual growth rate of 17.5 per cent for total external debt and 11 per cent for foreign direct investment (IMF, 1983, Table 27). As a result, in the period 1973 to 1978, we can see the proportion of external finance to NOLDCs provided by commercial banks rising to 60 per cent of the total, with foreign direct investment and official finance falling to 18 and 19 per cent respectively. This trend continued in the years 1978 to 1980, with net external debt from private commercial sources rising to 70 per cent of the total. Most of the increase in the latter period was in the form of short-term loans (loans with a maturity of less than a year); these increased fivefold between 1978 and 1980 compared with a rise in long-term credit by just over half of its 1978 figure. Since 1981, the share of external credit from private sources has been falling

fairly quickly, with the use of Fund credit and foreign direct investment filling the gap.

For the non oil developing nations, sovereign loans as a percentage
of total private external debt ranged from between 51 per cent in 1973
to 68 per cent in 1983 (IMF, 1983, Table 32). Among the major
'problem' debtor countries, the proportion of sovereign external debt
was even higher.

Why have so many of the NOLDCs recently opted for such high
foreign gearing ratios and, more specifically, why did sovereign
borrowing become a popular means of external finance in the 1970s
compared with earlier periods when foreign direct investment was
more common? This question can only be answered satisfactorily
through further analysis of the components of the demand and supply
in the international credit markets.

On the demand side, it is useful to begin the analysis by making a
small diversion to explain the Modigliani–Miller (MM) theorem of
investment.[4] According to this theorem, if a firm's gearing ratio (debt
finance/equity finance) is plotted on the horizontal axis and the firm's
cost of capital on the vertical axis, then the line which is plotted will be
horizontal. The point is illustrated in Figure 1.1. From the standpoint
of capital costs, it is irrelevant whether the firm chooses a high or low
gearing ratio. This is in contrast to the traditional view of the shape of
the cost of capital curve, which was U-shaped. The reasoning behind
the MM theorem was that, if individual investors carried out their own
gearing, any change in the gearing ratio of the firm would be offset by
the activities of investors, who are assumed to have the same access to
capital markets and to pay the same rate of interest on loans as firms.
For example, if the firm increased the percentage of debt finance
through an increase in bond issues, then the effect of this on the cost of
capital would be offset by an equal and opposite action on the part
of individual investors, who would alter their 'home-made' gearing
ratios. Therefore, the firm's cost of capital will be unchanged, no
matter what its gearing ratio. To the practical financier, this may be
counter-intuitive. The theorem appears to ignore the real world fact
that the costs of capital are higher for highly geared firms because the
markets perceive them to be a riskier investment. The results of the
MM theorem stem from two rather special assumptions. First, that all
agents have equal access to the capital markets and borrow at the same
rate of interest and, secondly, that there is no possibility of default by
firms. It is these assumptions, particularly the second, which rule out
the usefulness of this theorem as anything but an abstract piece of
theory. But although it has little practical use, it is valuable because it
isolates the factors that will give rise to a U-shaped cost of capital curve.

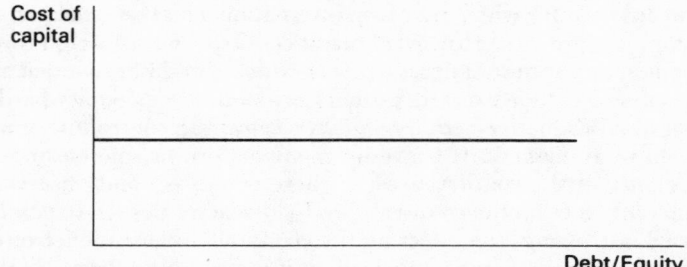

Figure 1.1   The Modigliani–Miller theorem.
Source: Modigliani and Miller (1958); see also Hay and Morris (1979).

The MM theorem may have greater applicability in the international capital markets with respect to the foreign gearing ratio chosen by a nation which is a net importer of capital. This is because default (defined as an outright repudiation of external debt obligations) has a probability that is close to zero in many countries. Unlike the bankrupt firm where there is a well-defined set of legal procedures which are enacted in the case of insolvency, for the defaulting debtor nation there is no such set of procedures. Historically, countries that have defaulted on the external debt obligations have been denied access to capital markets in the future until the default is made right. In the case of China, for example, there has been a strong suggestion that, in order to be allowed back on to the international capital markets, it must meet its external obligations dating back to 1949, when the country defaulted on its external debt. Although the number of outright repudiations has been very low, such a repudiation is a possibility. The country considering repudiation has to weigh its costs against the benefits. This point receives further consideration in Chapter 3. But it is possible to say that, using historical precedent as the basis for predictions, the probability of outright repudiation by a country is very low when compared with the case of repudiation by a firm. Therefore, the MM theorem may have more applicability in the sovereign loan case than in any other case. That is, for the developing nation, the foreign gearing ratio it chooses may not influence its cost of foreign capital curve.

However, there are other factors influencing the decision to be highly geared which do not fit neatly into any economic theory. Net imports of capital increase the interdependence of the borrowing country. That is, if the country relies on foreign capital markets for economic development, it loses some economic sovereignty. This is true of any country which trades on international markets, not just the developing countries. However, many countries view foreign direct investment as, at best, a necessary evil which should be avoided if at all possible. Foreign direct investment involves foreign equity participation in a productive activity and, typically, the controlling shares are held by foreigners. It has a direct impact on the microeconomic sovereignty of the country because there is a direct and observable foreign influence on the country's productive activities. In the case of external borrowing, the effect on the economic independence of the country is not so apparent, especially if it is a sovereign loan which is not project-specific. Unless the country gets into debt servicing difficulties, the lender will not interfere with the application of the loan to a particular use. On the demand side, this is probably the main explanation why there was such a sudden change in the gearing ratios of many developing countries during the 1970s. No nation could foresee the loss of macroeconomic sovereignty that has occurred through IMF intervention in these economies, something which is an integral part of the rescheduling packages. I return to this issue in Chapter 5. In order to see why the majority of external debt was in the form of sovereign external loans as opposed to private non-guaranteed debt, it is necessary to analyse the events on the supply side of the analysis.

The developing nations could not have altered their foreign gearing ratios in such a dramatic way had the supply of lending to these countries not been forthcoming. The Western nations are characterized by well-developed capital markets and an excess supply of capital. Until the mid-1970s, however, direct lending to the developing nations made up about 30 per cent of the total of external financing to NOLDCs. Then, as will be noted from the figures cited earlier, the proportion rose very rapidly to a peak of 70 per cent. There were two reasons why a sudden increase occurred in the supply of credit in the form of private foreign loans to developing countries. First, the emergence of the Euromarkets in the 1960s added a new dimension to international capital flows. The reasons for the growth of the Euromarkets are well documented[5] and will not be elaborated upon here. For our purposes, the important point is that this development transformed the international economy from one where capital flows between countries were largely immobile across national boundaries (except via foreign direct investment) to one where capital was highly mobile and traded on the Euromarkets. Secondly, there was the sudden growth in balance of payments surpluses of most of the member nations of OPEC, a consequence of the oil price hikes of the 1970s. In the period 1974 to 1980, a total of $317 billion in cash surplus accrued to the oil-exporting developing nations. Of this amount, $47 billion went to developing countries in the form of direct finance, but $147 billion (more than 50 per cent) was deposited in private Western banks (IMF, 1981, Table 22). These deposits were channelled to developing countries in the form of sovereign loans via the Euromarkets.

A final question which remains relates to the fact that a rising proportion of private external debt was publicly guaranteed or made directly to governments rather than being in the form of direct, non publicly guaranteed lending. As was pointed out in the Introduction, non publicly guaranteed foreign loans suffer from a number of disadvantages when contrasted with domestic loans made to a domestic-based firm. Although responsibility for repayment lies with an individual firm rather than with a sovereign nation, the cross-border nature of the loan means the lender is potentially subject to political interference by the host government, especially if the borrower defaults and the 'foreign' private bank attempts to acquire assets in a way similar to that it would use to foreclose upon a debtor inside its own national boundaries. Also, the imposition of exchange controls could make the repatriation of the private capital difficult. Now contrast this with a sovereign loan. In this case, the ultimate responsibility for its repayment rests with a government. If it is assumed that countries cannot go bankrupt, then the only risk faced by the lender relates to the probability of outright repudiation. As was noted earlier, this has been an extremely rare event in international capital markets. If the two types of lending are compared in this way, it is not surprising that private banks opted for sovereign lending rather than non-guaranteed private lending. At the time, they did not appear to consider the possibility that, even though it might be difficult to declare a country technically in default, it could none the less encounter very serious debt-servicing problems. This point is raised again at several stages in this book.

This completes the review of the determinants of international capital flows and, in particular, sovereign borrowing and lending. The next section discusses the origins of the current international financial problems.

The Origins of the Current International Debt Problems

The starting point for a study of the current international financial difficulties is a review of the magnitude of the external debts of developing nations.[6] As was noted earlier, there was a rapid growth in commercial lending (and sovereign loans) as a proportion of total external debt for developing countries. For the NOLDC group (defined on p. 3) total external debt grew by more than five times in the period 1973 to 1983 to reach a total of more than $669 billion, with estimates for 1984 put at $711 billion. This figure includes both long-term and short-term debt but excludes debt owed to the IMF. In terms of the percentage share of external debt for all developing countries, two groups need to be singled out for special attention:

(1) The NOLDCs accounted for 87 per cent of all developing country debt at the end of 1983.

(2) The 'group of 25', consisting of the 25 developing countries with the largest total external debt, accounted for 79 per cent of all developing country external debt at the end of 1983. This group is identified in Table 1.1, with the top five debtors listed first.

Not all the major debtor countries have had to reschedule their debt. Four of the countries listed in Table 1.1 also belong to the IMF classification of major oil exporters. These countries are Algeria, Venezuela, Nigeria and Indonesia. Two countries, Romania and Hungary, are part of the Eastern bloc nations and do not really fit the description of developing country, given their fairly extensive industrial base. As was noted earlier, the share of commercial bank loans in total external debt peaked at 70 per cent in the period 1978 to 1980 and more than half of this debt was in the form of sovereign loans.

For the NOLDCs, debt service (amortization on long-term debt plus interest on long-term and short-term debt) as a percentage of exports of goods and services rose from an average of 15.45 per cent in 1973 to 1977 to 25 per cent in 1981 to 1982. The rescheduling of external debt reduced this ratio to 22.5 per cent in 1982 to 1983. In 1984, it is estimated to have declined to 22 per cent. For the group of 25, the debt service ratio rose from 21.5 per cent in 1980 to 32.5 per cent in 1982, falling to 30 per cent in 1983, and is estimated to be at 29 per cent in 1984. The reason for the discrepancy between the two groups arises from the fact that, among the major debtors, a larger proportion of the loans consists of commercial loans subject to variable rates of interest. These countries were particularly hard hit by the rise in nominal rates of interest from the mid-1970s onward. In their cases the rapid rise in nominal rates accelerated the amortization of real debt and raised current debt-servicing obligations. This sudden increase in *front loading* meant the nations had to find the resources to meet these obligations. The front-loading problem receives more attention in Chapter 3.

Table 1.1   *The 'Group of 25' Developing Countries with the Largest Total External Debt*

Country	Total sovereign disbursed external debt at the end of 1983 ($ BN)
Brazil	79.58
Mexico	66.73
Argentina	24.59
Republic of Korea	23.07
Indonesia	21.77
Venezuela	21.43
Israel	17.85
India	15.89
Chile	15.53
Egypt	15.15
Yugoslavia	14.95
Turkey	13.66
Algeria	12.92
The Philippines	12.91
South Africa	11.76
Portugal	10.67
Nigeria	10.52
Thailand	9.73
Malaysia	9.50
Peru	9.45
Pakistan	8.15
Morocco	7.93
Romania	7.58
Colombia	6.57
Hungary	N/A

Source: World Bank *World Debt Tables*, 1984–5.

Another feature of the current situation was the rapid rise in short-term loans as a percentage of total external obligations. For the NOLDCs, this represented 8.7 per cent of total external debt in 1973, but the percentage rose rapidly from the late 1970s to peak at 20 per cent in 1982. The rescheduling packages have reduced this share, because the maturity of the short-term debt has been extended beyond a year. It was estimated to have declined to 12.5 per cent by 1984.

This rapid rise in short-term debt was a signal that all was not well for the developing countries. Earlier (p. 3), we said that the primary reason for importing capital was to finance growth and development.

From the standpoint of the international lender and borrower, imported capital should be used to finance economic development in a country and loans should be made with this purpose in mind. The use of short-term debt for this purpose was incorrect because of the long-term nature of the income streams that will be used to finance the debt. Therefore, short-term lending for this purpose was sub-optimal. The question we must ask is whether the developing nations were borrowing for purposes other than for development. The evidence suggests that they were. The remainder of this section is organized as follows: the empirical work by Cline (1984) and the IMF (1983, 1984) is integrated to illustrate why many developing countries suddenly increased their sovereign borrowing on world markets. It appears that, by the late 1970s, rather than borrowing to finance future growth rates they were borrowing as a means of solving increasing problems on the current account.

The Relationship Between the Growth of Current Account Deficits, External Debt and Random Economic Shocks

Before looking at the interrelationship between random shocks, the growth in the current account deficit and the rise of external debt, it is worth investing some time to dispel the notion that developing countries borrowed on international capital markets to finance consumption. The strongest critics of the developing country debt problem have argued that these nations used their external loans for consumption purposes rather than to finance productive investment activities. This claim, if valid, is important because it suggests that the external finance was being used for a purpose at odds with the economic reasons behind borrowing. However, there is no empirical evidence whatever to support this accusation. Beenstock (1984) uses cross-section country data (for the year 1977) to test the significance of the share of consumption in GNP as an explanation for the growth of external debt/GNP in developing countries. He finds the coefficient on this variable has the wrong sign and is not statistically significant. In an IMF survey (1983) of the twenty major debtor countries, a steady rise is found in the share of investment in national income throughout the 1970s. For this group, the investment as a percentage of GNP rose from an average of 18.9 per cent between 1968 and 1972 to an average of 23.6 per cent between 1978 and 1981. Furthermore, the IMF finds that even in countries with rising current account deficits, the savings ratio showed a reasonably strong performance. These figures are not indicative of countries 'borrowing to consume'. The reasons behind the growing indebtedness are far more complex.

The rest of this section is devoted to an analysis of these reasons.

The IMF (1983, 1984) has presented evidence on the growth of the current account deficits of the NOLDCs and the 25 major debtors. For the NOLDCs, current account deficits rose by $67 billion in the period 1978 to 1981. In the early part of the 1970s the growth rate had been far less rapid and did not follow a steady upward trend. At the end of 1973 the current account deficit stood at $11.3 billion. In 1974 and 1975 it rose fairly rapidly to peak at $46.3 billion in 1975. In 1976 and 1977 it fell off to amounts of $32.6 billion and $28.9 billion, respectively. The IMF (1983, p. 69) attributes the rapid growth rate in the late 1970s (a trend which was not reversed until 1982) to several factors:

(1)   More than one-third of the rise was due to an increase in *net* interest payments, the excess of interest payments on external debt over interest received on reserves and other financial assets. This is explained by both the increase in outstanding debt, which had occurred through the 1970s, and the rate of interest paid on this debt. Most of the new loans negotiated in the 1970s were subject to floating rates of interest. For NOLDCs, the percentage share of total debt subject to variable rates of interest rose from 7 per cent in 1973 to 37 per cent in 1982. This figure reached 42 per cent for the 25 major debtors by 1982 and for some of the Latin American debtors in this group was more than 75 per cent.

(2)   World recession in the 1970s: the first oil price shock at the end of 1973 was responsible for a subsequent recession in the industrialized countries. Because the First World is a major market for developing country exports, this had the effect of reducing export revenues in these countries. By 1975, the current account deficit as a percentage of exports for NOLDCs was 30 per cent. The subsequent strong recovery in the West had the effect of significantly improving export markets and the prices of primary commodities, so that the current account deficits of this group underwent a considerable improvement as the figures cited earlier reveal. Unfortunately it was short-lived, because the subsequent rise in oil prices in late 1978 induced a second world recession, from which recovery has to date been far less marked. This weakened the demand for exports from NOLDCs and had a severe impact on the prices for primary commodities between 1980 and 1983. The result was a sizeable deterioration (13 per cent) in the NOLDC terms of trade (the ratio of the export price index to the import price index) between 1979 and 1982. In 1983, it improved slightly. For the developing countries who were net oil importers, the deterioration of the terms of trade was 20 per cent between 1979 and 1982, recovering by 1.75 per cent in 1983.

(3)   The comments made under (2) were quite general and did not distinguish between the oil trade balance and the non oil trade balance. By making the distinction, it is possible to compute the percentage contribution of these factors to the current account balance. For the NOLDC non oil terms of trade, we see that between the years 1973 and 1975 there was a rise in the average export prices received by the group, which effectively wrote off 40 per cent of their external debt. In the period from 1981 to 1982, the trend had reversed and declining average export prices (in terms of US dollars) made real amortization of debt more rather than less difficult. The IMF (1983, p. 69) estimates that the decline in the non oil terms of trade was responsible for another one-third of the increase in the NOLDC current account deficit between 1978 and 1981. The appreciation of the US dollar also had a negative effect on debt servicing because most of the debt was denominated in US dollars.

(4)   The IMF (1983, p. 69) attributes more than a quarter of the increase in the current account deficit over the period cited to the adverse change in the group's oil trade balance, even though some of the countries in this group are net oil exporters.

While the IMF *World Economic Outlook* published in 1983 cites the decline in the oil trade balance as one of the factors responsible for the deterioration in the current account deficits of the NOLDC group in the late 1970s, in the 1984 version it comments that:

> there was no close correlation between the level of a country's dependence on imported oil and the extent of the deterioration in its current account. (p. 61)

This apparent inconsistency is not confined to the IMF studies. Beenstock (1984) explores the determinants of the growth of external debt on a country-by-country basis. He tests to see whether the share of oil imports in GNP is a significant variable in explaining the growth of external indebtedness of non oil exporting developing nations. The data come from a sample of 36 developing nations for the year 1977. He finds a positive relationship between the share of oil imports/GNP and the growth in indebtedness (D/GNP), but it is not statistically significant.

On the other hand, Cline (1984) cites the oil price increase in excess of US inflation in the period 1974 to 1982 (for net oil importing countries only) as one of the major contributing factors to the growth of external debt. The Cline figures refer to potential increases in debt as a result of the increase in oil prices. Cline is working with an unconstrained balance of payments model: the indebtedness of a country is determined by the growth of the current account deficit with no specified finance constraint. Cline calculates the import bill of these countries under the oil prices of the 1970s and compares these figures with what the bill would have been had the price of oil not risen faster than the US wholesale price index. Therefore, his computations are an indirect way of measuring the effect of oil price increases on the growth of external debt. Further, Cline's results have not taken into account the domestic adjustment programmes undertaken by individual developing countries in response to the sudden rise in the import bill. This, and the indirectness of the approach, is the probable explanation for the discrepancy between the Cline and Beenstock results. Beenstock's direct estimation procedure is using cross-section country data from one year and, therefore, would have picked up the effects of any adjustment programme.

Clearly the impact of oil prices on external indebtedness is an issue that has not been resolved in the empirical literature. Although we would probably side with the Beenstock results because they are the product of a stronger empirical test, we should not ignore the impact of oil prices on the growth of the world economy, which in turn affected the current account balances of the developing countries via the impact of export revenues. Nor should we ignore the link between the rise in the price of oil and the subsequent decline in the prices of other primary commodities as industrial demand for these declined. When considering the impact of the oil price hikes, the developing countries need to be divided into three groups. First, there are the net oil importers who undertook adjustment policies, altering their consumption and investment patterns so that the import bill from the oil price rise was substantially reduced. For this group the impact of the oil price shock was largely indirect via the effect on the world economy. Secondly, there were the net oil importers who undertook little in the way of adjustment policy and therefore continued to suffer from high import bills. In the case of the second group the impact of the rising price of oil on current account deficits was both direct and indirect. These differences in adjustment policies are not confined to the developing nations. While countries like Japan and those in Western Europe opted for rapid adjustment to the change in the relative price of oil, the United States was much slower to adjust.

Finally, there are the net oil exporters not in capital surplus. These countries borrowed on the expectation of higher future income streams from oil revenues, that is, they borrowed to finance future growth and development. This in turn led to rising external debt and, as the price of oil began to fall and real interest rates turned positive in the late 1970s, current account deficits began to rise.

In conclusion, the IMF and other studies point to four factors contributing to rising current account deficits from the late 1970s until 1983: the world recession; the rise in net interest payments; the decline in the prices of primary commodities (oil excepted); the rise in the price of oil, the effect of which depended on the country. These factors must be interpreted as *random exogenous economic shocks* to the world economy. They are termed shocks because the figures for these factors deviated significantly from their postwar trend values. The unpredictability of the shocks made them random. They are exogenous because they were outside any single economic system, that is they did not result from the action of any one system. These shocks had an impact on the industrialized countries as well, but in these cases (with the odd minor exception) there was no large and growing external debt to add to their problems.

Cline (1984, Table 1.4, p. 13) attempts to attach some numbers to the effect of each of the same external shocks on the growth of NOLDC debt. When related to the study by the IMF between the growth of current account deficits as a result of the same shocks, a story begins to emerge. The random shocks created serious balance of payments problems for developing countries, and they attempted to deal with the problem by increasing capital inflows through international borrowing. Cline notes that total external debt for this group increased by $482 billion in the period 1973 to 1982. He attributes a large part (54 per cent) of this increase to the oil price shocks, although there is reason to be sceptical about this figure, a point noted earlier. Cline computes the percentage contribution of the other 'shocks' as follows:

(1) A real interest rate (1981, 1982) in excess of the average for 1961 to 1980: approximately 9 per cent.

(2) Terms of trade loss, 1981 to 1982: approximately 16 per cent.

(3) World recession – export volume loss in 1981 to 1982: approximately 4 per cent.

Cline stresses one should not conclude that 83 per cent of the increase in debt can be explained by these four shocks. The measures are indirect and obtained through an unconstrained balance of payments approach. The computations ignore the individual adjustment policies adopted by developing countries in response to these shocks. This is rather a strong assumption and rules out using the figures as anything but a very rough guide. However, his is the only published work that attempts to quantify the link between the growth in external debt and the random shocks to the world economy. It is noteworthy that the figures cited for the three random shocks other than oil relate to the early part of the 1980s. This underlines the point that, until the late 1970s when developing nations began to experience rapid rises in their current account deficits, their reasons for borrowing were on the whole 'healthy' in that they were importing capital to finance development. This issue is elaborated upon below.

The evidence cited above points to a very rapid rise in the current account deficits of the NOLDCs from 1978 to 1981. However, the growth in external indebtedness began much earlier. At the beginning of this chapter (p. 5), it was noted that private long-term debt to NOLDCs increased at an average annual rate of 25.5 per cent from 1974 to 1983. The growth in external debt up to 1978 was consistent with the economic determinants of international capital flows (cited on pp. 1–9). Until 1978 real rates of interest were negative and, therefore, if the developing country's marginal productivity from the domestic endowment of capital was greater than zero, it made economic sense to borrow on international capital markets to finance economic growth. We have also noted (p. 9) the willingness of lenders to supply these funds, particularly if they were in the form of sovereign loans. Therefore, the reasons for the rapid growth rates in external debt were not in any way worrying. The rapid growth rates are explained by both demand and supply side-factors: capital was abundant, the price of credit low, so why not finance development via Euromarket loans? The only exception to this argument was in the period following the first round of oil price increases. In this case, the shock to the balance of payments of some of the net oil importers probably caused them to increase their borrowing to finance at least part of the import bill. However, this response varied so much among the different countries that it is difficult to argue that this 'hiccough' was responsible for subsequent debt-servicing problems. Also, the impact on the current account deficits was short-lived because of the strong recovery in the industrial countries after 1975.

Hence, we may conclude that, until 1978, borrowing by developing nations had been for reasonably healthy reasons, with the possible exception of the 12 to 14 months after the rise in oil prices in late 1973. But, while the reasons for the increase in capital inflows were sound, a point of concern was the increase in the foreign gearing ratios of the developing countries. Unlike other forms of capital inflows, increasing amounts of external debt would make these countries vulnerable to future shocks and interfere with their ability to service this debt. Between 1978 and 1981 the concern over high gearing was supplemented by a more serious problem: the use of external debt to finance increasing current account deficits, which in turn were largely the result of random shocks to the world economy.

Up to this point, the period to 1981 has been discussed. Since 1981 the current account balance for NOLDCs has improved. The IMF presents an interesting table (Table 111–2, p. 49) in their 1984 edition of *World Economic Outlook*. The table divides the NOLDC group into oil exporters and oil importers and attempts to disaggregate the recent changes in the overall current account balance into the oil trade balance, net interest payments, the cyclical element in the non oil terms of trade and a residual, interpreted by the IMF as the influence of domestic adjustment policies. Scrutiny of the table suggests that, for NOLDCs as a whole, the cyclical factor (stemming from world recession) and net interest payments continued to exert a significant negative influence on the current account deficits of these countries in 1982 and 1983. The negative effects of the oil trade balance were reduced for the net oil importers in this group. For the NOLDCs, the residual component improved by an amount greater than the improvement in the current account balance taken as a whole in the period 1981 to 1983. If the IMF is correct in using the residual component as a proxy for adjustment policies, then it suggests that domestic policies adopted by these countries have had a favourable effect in reducing the size of the current account deficits.

Domestic Policies in Debtor Countries

The previous section stressed the role of exogenous shocks to the world economy as an explanation of the growth of external debt over the past decade. Some readers may be wondering whether domestic policies adopted by the different debtor nations affected the ability of the countries to withstand the shocks. There is some evidence to suggest this is the case. The IMF (1983, pp. 137–40) has looked at this question by comparing the domestic policies of the NOLDC group. The IMF attempted to illustrate that countries in this group which followed restrictive fiscal and credit policies and realistic exchange rates had more favourable current account developments (and hence did not require external sources of finance to the same degree) than countries which were more relaxed about domestic policy.

To evaluate the economic performance of the NOLDCs, the IMF used five economic indicators:

– the real GDP growth rate
– the change in the rate of growth of real GDP
– the change in inflation

– the change in the current account balance in relation to the export of goods and services
– the change in the 'adjusted' current account balance; it was adjusted to exclude all external influences.

The number of extreme observations in the data caused the IMF to use medians rather than weighted averages. They divide the countries into two groups:

(1)   The 'high' group: in this classification are all the countries with economic indicators above the median. They typically experienced expansion in fiscal deficits in the period 1979/80 to 1981/82 of 3.5 per cent of GDP and an appreciation of their real effective exchange rates of 9 per cent per annum. The real effective exchange rate is an import weighted exchange rate index multiplied by the ratio of the domestic consumer price index to the import weighted consumer price index of the country's major trading partners. For a complete explanation of this index, the reader is referred to the introduction of the IMF monthly publication, *International Financial Statistics* (IFS).

(2)   The 'low' group: these countries had economic indicators that fell below the median. They typically experienced a contraction of fiscal deficits of approximately 1 per cent of GDP from 1979/80 to 1981/82 and a depreciation of their real effective exchange rate of 1.5 per cent per annum.

The IMF came up with a number of interesting observations. First, there was a positive association (note that this was not a statistically significant association) between a change in a fiscal deficit and a change in the current account deficits. Those countries in the high group showed median increases in their current account deficits equal to 14.5 per cent of their exports of goods and services. The low group experienced median declines in their fiscal and current account deficits equal to 1.5 per cent of exports. Some economists would argue that the direction of causation runs from the current account deficit to the fiscal deficit because the openness of these economies subjects them to wide fluctuations in export earnings, which in turn undermines their tax base. However, the IMF study found no evidence to indicate this was the relevant direction of causation.

It might be expected that the tight policies of the low group which helped to correct their external balances may have acted as an impediment to their real economic growth rates. The IMF finds no evidence to confirm this. However, the period studied is very short and the full impact on growth rates may not have been felt at the time of the review.

The IMF also studied the performance of the real effective exchange rate in relation to rates of economic growth and current account performance. The low group with relatively depreciating exchange rates was found to have (compared to the high group with appreciating real effective exchange rates) significantly higher growth rates and significantly smaller increases in current account deficits.

Although the period studied by the IMF is too short for any hard-and-fast rules to be drawn, the findings do suggest that countries can undertake domestic adjustment policies in order to weather the economic storm caused by shocks to the world economy. The findings are not at all surprising. If countries deal with a balance of payments disequilibrium by allowing their real effective exchange rates to depreciate, their dependence on capital imports to offset the current account deficit will be less marked than countries which artificially support their exchange rates. Also, countries which cut back on fiscal expenditure and so lower their import bill (because the implied reduction in domestic demand will affect imports) will decrease their deficit on the current account and reduce the need to import capital.

The Declining Role of the IMF

The main argument of this section centres around the idea that, by the late 1970s, a number of random shocks had caused severe current account problems for many of the developing nations, especially those that had grown to be highly geared in foreign debt in the more favourable climate of the early 1970s. This in turn prompted more external borrowing, and the continued pressure on terms of trade and the debt burden via high real rates of interest forced many countries into a rescheduling crisis by 1982. The question the reader may be asking is how did countries deal with serious balance of payments problems prior to the growth of capital mobility brought about by the development of the Euromarkets? It was not until the late 1960s that the Euromarkets facilitated the growth of private commercial bank lending to developing nations; before this time, it had been a relatively small proportion of total external debt (see p. 8). Yet there were balance of payments problems arising in earlier periods and they were not confined to developing countries, as Britain's experience in 1976 will remind the reader.

The answer to this apparent inconsistency lies in the role of the IMF. At the 1944 conference at Bretton Woods, the IMF articles of agreement assigned to the Fund a number of important responsibilities. Southard (1979) summarizes the primary objective of the IMF:

to assist members to finance their balance of payments deficits and to monitor their exchange rate and policies. (p. 15)

To achieve its objectives, the Fund assumed two functions. Under the adjustable peg exchange rate system which prevailed until 1972, the IMF had the power to approve or order changes in par values if the problem underlying a member's balance of payments difficulties was deemed to be one of 'fundamental disequilibrium', i.e. a country's external balance was incompatible with full employment and free trade in goods and services. Secondly, if the problems were not of a fundamental nature, members were granted access to the financial resources of the IMF to help see them through the difficulties. Today the Fund resources include credit tranches, the compensating financing facility, the extended facility, provisions for buffer stock and supplementary financing, the reserve tranche, and special drawing rights (SDRs). The last two facilities have conditions attached to their use: the borrowed resources must be repaid within a specified period of time and the IMF has to approve a programme of adjustment before the facilities can be used.

Given that balance of payments problems have, in the postwar period, been the primary responsibility of the IMF, we would have expected to see the Fund intervening when the developing countries began to experience serious current account problems from 1978 onward. However, this was not the case. Between 1978 and 1980, the average share of Fund credit as a percentage of external finance (for NOLDCs) was 2 per cent, rising to 7 per cent in 1981. It was not until 1982, four years after the current account problems began, that this percentage share rose to 20 per cent. In place of the IMF, we observe the use of the international capital markets to deal with these problems. Once capital had become mobile to the degree allowed by the Euro-markets, the power of the IMF to fulfil its responsibilities began to be eroded and was further undermined as the international economy moved to a fully flexible exchange rate system. Before 1972, the IMF would have intervened much earlier had there been the random shocks to the world economy, which in turn would have had serious implications for the current account deficits of the developing nations. As it was, the international capital markets filled a role that previously would have been the responsibility of the IMF.

External Debts in Industrialized Countries

Recently, the growing net external debt of a number of industrialized countries has given cause for concern. In late 1984, the United States became a net foreign debtor, that is, the claims held by US residents on foreigners are now less than their liabilities to foreigners. At the end of 1985, the external financial debt of the United States is estimated to rise to $500 billion, excluding all direct investment and netting out official gold holdings and reserves held in foreign currencies. Other net foreign debtors include the Scandinavian countries, Greece, Spain, Portugal and Ireland, though it is doubtful whether the last four countries can be strictly classified as industrialized.

This raises the question of why First World nations are net foreign debtors. Since it is the growth and size of the US foreign debt that is of central concern, this question is answered in the context of the US debt situation. Clearly the US borrowing requirements cannot be explained by a development cycle hypothesis. However, the US case illustrates a now familiar story. The US has been running an increasing current account deficit since the third quarter of 1982. This is closely linked to the rising fiscal deficit: in 1985, the $200 billion fiscal deficit will be largely financed by a current account deficit estimated to reach $150 billion. The current account deficit has in turn been financed by large inflows of foreign capital – these turned the United States into a net foreign debtor by the end of 1984. The international capital markets have been only too willing to meet US foreign borrowing requirements, a point underlined by the relative strength of the US dollar until the first quarter of 1985.

However, there are important differences between the US case and that of the developing country debtor nations. None of the US net foreign debt takes the form of sovereign loans made by the Western private banking system. Of the total US government debt at the end of 1984, 19 per cent is held by US commercial banks and other financial institutions and 14 per cent by foreign and international organizations.[7] Further, almost all of the foreign debt (public and private) is in some form of negotiable debt and, therefore, can be traded on the international financial markets.

Another difference is that the United States has incurred the external debt in its own currency, unlike the developing nations, which had their external loans denominated in (largely) US dollars. With investors assuming the exchange rate risk, the USA will not face a sudden increase in the currency value of its debt.

The differences noted above make any detailed discussion of the US external debt problems inappropriate for a book focusing on sovereign risk analysis. However, the importance of the USA to the world economy means that any policies it adopts to curb the growth in external indebtedness will have implications for the rest of the world. For example, although depreciation of the dollar would reduce the currency value of developing country external debt, recession in the USA and the improved international competitiveness of US firms could depress the export earnings of these countries.

Historical Precedents

In this section the historical precedents for the current international financial problems are briefly reviewed. Debt-servicing difficulties on the part of borrowing nations are nothing new. In Chapter 4 of his book, *The Migration of British Capital to 1875* (1927), L. H. Jenks describes US and Mexican payment problems in the 1840s. During 1841 and 1842 nine American states stopped paying interest on their sovereign debts, which took the form of state bond issues. Three of the states declared that they would not repay their debts. Mississippi and Michigan claimed they were not responsible for these debts because they had been contracted in an 'unconstitutional manner' (Jenks, 1927, p. 103) and Florida appealed to its minority status because at this time it was officially a ward of the government. A few years later, dividends were resumed by the other six states. Mexico had, by the early 1840s, £50 million worth of government stocks (again mainly in the form of bonds) which were in default, with unpaid dividends overdue by between five and twenty years (Jenks, 1927, p. 115).

The account by W. A. Lewis (1978) of international financial problems in the 1890s could be equally applied to many of the current international financial problems. Lewis remarks that:

> As we approach 1890, the problems of the borrowers intensify. The steady fall in prices continually increased the real burden of debt, irrespective of the terms of trade. Prices of imports were coming down with the prices of exports but the contractual obligations of interest and amortization remained the same. The fall in prices was so pronounced that the average for the boom was lower than the average for the preceding trough. . . There seemed to be no end to the continual fall in the prices of primary products. Then there was the gloom spread by the Baring crisis, the associated default of Argentina, and Australia's difficulties in meeting her payments. . .
> (Lewis, 1978, pp. 179–80)

This passage suggests the causes of debt-servicing difficulties are nothing new and points to well-intentioned debtor countries getting into trouble. The Australian financial system finally collapsed in 1893.

Turning to the 1900s, there are more examples of countries encountering repayment problems with respect to their external debt. Following the revolution, Russia defaulted on foreign bond holdings and these debts are still outstanding. A crisis in Argentina in the latter half of 1913 was characterized by a rapid outflow of gold and a large number of commercial failures.

On the other hand, the ratios of external debt to trade were high for a good number of countries which did not encounter serious debt-servicing problems, including Australasia (480 per cent), Canada (860 per cent), South Africa (630 per cent), Japan (230 per cent) and China (220 per cent).[8] These figures indicate that high percentages do not necessarily cause a country to repudiate or postpone its debt repayments. The problem of using this type of ratio is discussed at length in Chapter 2.

During the Great Depression of the 1930s, many of the governments of the poorer nations defaulted on their external debts. By 1935 the 'default status' of the American-held portions of Latin American external loans was as shown in Table 1.2. This table illustrates that, as recently as the 1930s, there were Latin American debt problems. The term default status is used here because, although payments were suspended for a period, there was resumption of repayment in certain cases.

Bareau (1983) attempted to draw parallels between the international debt problems provoked by the German financial crisis of the 1930s and the current problems. However, we must be wary of such a comparison because the German problems differed on the supply or demand side, depending on whether one is considering Germany's long-term or short-term external debt obligations. With respect to the former, most of this debt was contracted by the German nation

Table 1.2 *Default Status in 1935 of the American-Held Portions of Latin American External Loans*

Country	Percentage of American loans to the country in default status
Argentina	24%
Brazil	93%
Chile	100%
Colombia	100%
Cuba	63%
Mexico	100%
Peru	100%
Other	77%

through the Dawes and Young Plans of, respectively, 1924 and 1930. The plans were drawn up in response to the need to reconsider the war reparations payments demanded by the Allies after the First World War and set by the Reparations Commission in May 1921. Both plans included a substantial loan to the German nation in an attempt to ease the burden of the reparations payments. However, the loans were floated in a number of international capital markets with the objective of selling them to individual investors. The non-German private Western banks were only indirectly involved. The Hoover moratorium (1931) and the subsequent Lausanne conference (1933) effectively put an end to the reparations payments; there was no default or rescheduling of these loans.

The situation in relation to short-term debt was a little different. Non-German private banks, especially those in London, were directly involved in granting short-term loans and acceptance credits. But the borrowers were the large German banks, which on lent the funds to German firms. Therefore, the short-term external debt, which stood at 12 billion reichsmarks by July 1931, had none of the features of a sovereign loan. Repayment of the debt was threatened by the collapse of the Danatbank in July 1931, which necessitated a two-day closure of all German banks. When the banks reopened, the withdrawal of foreign deposits was prohibited and exchange controls imposed. A subsequent meeting in London of creditor banks resulted in an agreement to reschedule the short-term external debt for six months; these 'standstill' agreements were the means by which default was averted.

This brief review of the history of international financial problems suggests that from the standpoint of the borrowing countries (the demand side of international capital flows) little has changed. Shocks to commodity prices and world recession have in the past impaired the ability of countries or state governments to meet their external debt obligations. The only difference relates to the decline in outright repudiations. China defaulted in 1949, Cuba in 1961 and North Korea in 1974. Until the middle of the 1900s such defaults were more frequent.

However, there is a fundamental difference on the supply side of international capital flows when we compare the current international financial problems with historical difficulties. In the current situation there are a great number of private Western commercial banks which are highly exposed in sovereign debt. As was noted in the earlier sections of this chapter, commercial bank lending became the dominant form of external finance to developing countries in the 1970s. One only has to examine the loan exposure of the five largest American banks in relation to their equity in order to observe the relatively high exposure of the Western banking system. In Table 1.3, the exposure is cited in relation to three of the problem debtor countries, Brazil, Mexico and Argentina.

Equivalent figures for British banks are more difficult to come by because the disclosure rules for this system are not as strict as for the American system. However, the figures convey to the reader some idea of how highly exposed many major banks are in this type of debt. This is the distinguishing feature of the current international financial problems.

For a historical precedent of sovereign lending by private banks, we have to go back to the fifteenth and sixteenth centuries. In 1494, the Medici Bank collapsed after a long period of decline. Sovereign loans had been made to the Pope, the Duke of Milan, Charles of Burgundy, and Edward IV of England, all of whom repudiated their debts. In the sixteenth century the Fugger Bank was highly exposed in sovereign lending to the Habsburg emperors, but in 1650 the bank had to write off this debt. However, there are crucial differences between the problems of these early merchant banks and the current situation. The sovereign borrowing was confined to a few banks and there was no interdependency of the international banking system of the sort that exists today. This last point is elaborated upon in Chapter 5.

Until 1913 Western commercial banks played no role in lending to developing nations. Their contribution remained a minor one until the emergence of the Euromarkets in the 1960s and the rapid growth of these markets in the 1970s. In the earlier periods, flows of international capital took the form of bond and equity financing, with London acting as the centre for these activities. The foreign bonds

Table 1.3   *Loan Exposure of the Top Five American Banks at the End of 1983 (millions of $US)*

Bank	Equity	Loans to Brazil	Mexico	Argentina
Citicorp	5,771	4,600	3,000	NA
Bank of America	5,136	2,484	2,471	NA
Chase Manhattan	3,051	2,560	1,553	800
Manufacturers Hanover Trust (MHT)	2,671	2,130	1,915	1,321
JP Morgan	3,069	1,785	1,174	741

Source: The Financial Times, 25 May 1984.

tended to be government or industry related bonds, such as those issued for the railways.

Therefore, the current situation exhibits a distribution of risks on the supply side of foreign lending which is quite different from any of the historical cases. Previous defaults by governments affected individual investors or banks, not an entire banking system. The interdependency of the banking system means that the failure of one major Western bank as a result of debt repudiation by sovereign lenders could well strain the international financial system to breaking point. This problem is discussed in some detail in Chapter 5 and will not be elaborated upon here. In the past, default by sovereign lenders did not threaten the international financial system the way it could today. Individual investors in the West were badly stung by the historical cases of default or suspension of payments, and no doubt this dampened the activities of the international financial markets at the time. However, the stability of the international banking system was not seriously undermined. In this sense the current sovereign debt problem is unique. The policy implications of this are discussed in Chapter 5.

Conclusions

This chapter began with an examination of the determinants of international capital flows and an exploration of the current international financial problems. Figures were cited to illustrate the rapid growth rate in the external debt of developing countries during the 1970s. Most significant was the growth in the percentage share of this debt owed to Western commercial banks. One of the themes of this chapter was that, by the end of the 1970s, developing nations were having to borrow to finance their growing current account deficits, which in turn were a consequence of a number of random economic shocks to the world economy. The interrelationship between the growth of NOLDC current account deficits, their external debt and random shocks was discussed in some detail. At the heart of the problem on the borrowing (demand) side was the negative impact of the random shocks, though there is some evidence to suggest that domestic adjustment policies undertaken by some countries did reduce their need to borrow.

The supply side of international capital flows was also affected by these shocks. With the growth of the Euromarkets and new forms of international mobile capital, the intervention role of the IMF underwent a considerable decline. The final section illustrated the historical precedent for sovereign borrowing problems, but stressed that the exposure in sovereign lending by the international banking system has little in the way of a historical parallel.

Notes: Chapter 1

1. For simple versions of the permanent income hypothesis see any inter- mediate macroeconomic textbook. For the original version see M. Fried- man, 1957.
2. See Appendix B, IMF, 1983.
3. The figures cited in the next few paragraphs are taken from IMF, 1983, 1984.
4. See Modigliani and Miller, 1958. For a thorough explanation of this and related issues see Hay and Morris, 1979.
5. See Johnson, 1983.
6. This section is able to draw on data from three main sources: IMF, 1983, 1984; World Bank, 1984; Cline, 1984. The use of extensive amounts of original data (for example, on world economy growth rates, oil prices, exchange rates, etc.) is avoided because such an exercise would repeat the excellent work cited and obscure the main points being made in this section.
7. From IMF, 1985, p. 481, l. 88.
8. See Lewis, 1978, p. 177.

2 A Review of Current Approaches to Sovereign Risk Analysis

This chapter is devoted to a critical review of the standard approaches to sovereign risk analysis. It is divided into three parts. The first section reviews the approaches to sovereign risk adopted by two of the popular financial magazines, *Euromoney* and *Institutional Investor*. In the next section, the statistical approaches to sovereign risk analysis are surveyed. Much of this literature comes from academic publications that do not have a wide readership among practising international bankers. None the less, the models developed in the academic literature are used by a wide range of international banks, either directly or indirectly through an economics appraisal service.[1] However, the technical nature of the academic publications has meant the practitioner has little understanding of the fundamental principles behind these models. In addition, there is no comparison of the results of the different studies and, most important, there is little in the way of criticism of these models. We have attempted to rectify these deficiencies, explaining the models in a way that readers with a weak background in economics and statistics can understand, and focusing on the two statistical approaches that have been used in this field: discriminant and logit analysis. This excludes one other approach,[2] but it was felt that this could be omitted without loss of generality. Finally, we return to the more practical side of sovereign risk analysis by reviewing the results of a recent survey on how banks assess sovereign risk. This final section lays the groundwork for the more general approach introduced in Chapter 3.

Financial Journals and Sovereign Risk Analysis

Two well-known financial journals, *Euromoney* and *Institutional Investor*, provide their readers with annual country rankings designed to be indicators of creditworthiness. The methodology employed is quite different in the two cases and, for this reason, they are reviewed separately.

Euromoney produces an annual Country Risk League Table which first appeared in the October 1979 publication (see Bance, 1978). The table ranks sovereign borrowers active in the Eurocurrency markets on the basis of the average weighted spread the country was able to obtain in a given year. The formula for the determination of a country's average weighted spread is:

$$\text{Average Weighted Spread} = \frac{\Sigma \,(\text{Volume} \times \text{Spread} \times \text{Maturity})}{\Sigma \,(\text{Volume} \times \text{Maturity})}$$

where

Σ = a summation sign.

Volume = all the loans signed for a given country in a given year on the Eurodollar and DM syndicated loan markets.

Spread = the spread or margin over LIBOR, the London Interbank Offered Rate.

Maturity = the time over which the loan matures.

Average weighted spreads are computed for all participating countries. The higher the spread, the greater the indication of riskiness. Those countries with low spreads are ranked highest in the league table. For example, in the country league table published in 1980, New Zealand was ranked as the best credit risk while, in 1979, the best risks were France and China. Brazil was ranked 47th out of 75 countries and Venezuela 22nd out of 75 countries in 1980. In 1979, Brazil had been ranked 42nd out of 66 and Venezuela 23rd. Mexico was ranked 28th out of 66 in 1979 but did not appear in the 1980 table.

Correspondents in the 'letters' pages of *Euromoney* have objected to the league table for a number of very good reasons. There are several problems with the methodology used to construct the table. First, the sample is self-selecting in that it only ranks countries active on the Euromarket in a given year. If countries do not participate in this market and/or they are excluded from it, the ranking will miss them out, even though these could be some of the riskier sovereign borrowers. Secondly, if the average spread over LIBOR changes in a given year then the ranking will be biased in favour of countries which borrowed before the increase in the spread, even though this has nothing to do with the riskiness of the individual borrower. Thirdly, the computation of average weighted spread assumes that spread and maturity are independent of each other, when in fact they are interdependent. Fourthly, the ranking ignores the possibility that fees may act as a partial substitute for higher spread. Finally, the method suggests that lenders always adjust for higher risk by raising the spread. However, for the risk-averse lender, who is faced with less than perfect information with respect to the borrowers, this may not be the case. If the lender always responded to higher risk by raising the spread, the deterrent effect would be greater for the low risk than the high risk borrower. At some point, the increase in spread will raise the average riskiness of the portfolio and lower expected returns. To prevent this from happening, the lender sets credit limits to deal with the risk/information problem rather than raising spreads. The league table ignores this possible response.

Since September 1982, *Euromoney* has published an extended version of the ranking described earlier. In this more recent computation, ease of access to all international capital markets (including the Eurobond market) is given a 40 per cent weight. Weights of 30 per cent are assigned, respectively, to the terms a country obtains in the syndicated loan market (or the terms a country 'would have received' if it did not borrow: see *Euromoney*, September 1982, p. 74) and the relative success of syndication. These modifications do not address the problems noted above.

To summarize, the rankings from the Country Risk League Table provide the analyst with an assessment of market attitudes toward sovereign borrowers through one variable, the average weighted spread. It cannot be interpreted as a measure of sovereign risk, because it gives no indication of the probability of default or rescheduling.

The *Institutional Investor* (II) also ranks developed and developing countries on a 'creditworthiness' table which is published twice a year in March and September. The rankings are based on a survey technique where 75 to 100 banks are asked to grade the creditworthiness of a country on a scale of 0 (the greatest probability of default) to 100 (the lowest probability of default). No bank ranks the country in which it has its headquarters. The responses are weighted according to the size of the bank's sovereign loan exposure and the 'sophistication' of its sovereign risk techniques. Readers are not given the weighting formula.

There are a number of problems with the 'banker judgement' approach. There is always going to be a subjective element in it because it relies on individual banker participation. For example, a banker may be reluctant to reveal his/her true judgement on the survey for fear that this information may become public. This is especially true if a certain bank is known to be highly exposed in sovereign lending to one or more countries. Also, there may be a problem arising with the assignation of heavier weights to highly exposed banks. Sovereign lending by a bank tends to be concentrated in one country or geographical area. The bank may only be highly sophisticated in the risk assessment that it does for the countries in which it is highly exposed; this expertise does not necessarily extend to all countries. Yet its relatively high exposure results in its responses on all countries being given a heavier weight.

Two academic studies have looked at the link between the II rating of countries and the spreads these countries are charged in the Euroloan markets. Angeloni and Short (1980) tested a number of explanatory variables for statistical significance with respect to Euro-currency spreads in 1978 and 1979. The II rating was found to be the most significant explanatory variable. Feder and Ross (1982) examined the correlation between the II rankings from the June/July 1979 survey and the spreads on Euromarket loans for the third quarter of 1979. The sample consisted of 78 loan transactions related to 38 countries. A simple test of association suggested a strong inverse relationship between the II rating a country received and the spread it was charged. More sophisticated econometric tests confirmed this relationship. However, these studies may be picking up subjective banker evaluation in both the market and in the rating. As such, the II rating is best interpreted as a reflection of market opinion rather than as an indicator of sovereign risk.

Statistical Models of Sovereign Risk Analysis

In the academic literature, the analysis of sovereign risk consists of the employment of statistical models to estimate the probability of default by a debtor nation. Treating the latter as the dependent variable, researchers have applied statistical methodology to the problem of identifying the significant independent or explanatory variables influencing the probability of default. Put simply, the problem is to estimate:

Probability of default $= f$ (economic variables)

where f is an abbreviation meaning 'function of'. If researchers could identify economic variables that influence the probability of default on sovereign lending, sovereign risk analysts would be able to track the variables over time with a view to identifying the countries most at risk of default. This part of Chapter 2 is divided into several sections: first, we review the variables commonly used in the statistical models of country risk; secondly, we describe the discriminant and logit models that have been employed in the estimating procedure; thirdly, the predictive ability of the models is discussed; finally, a critical summary is given of the problems that arise from the statistical approach.

Definition of Variables Used in Statistical Models of Sovereign Risk Analysis

DEPENDENT VARIABLE: PROBABILITY OF DEFAULT

The probability of default is the dependent variable that appears in the estimating equation. The researcher is trying to identify the economic variables that influence this dependent variable. Normally, we associate outright default with a borrower's repudiation of the debt. In the case of a sovereign borrower this would amount to the outright repudiation of the sovereign loan. However, these cases are quite rare. Though certain countries have threatened lenders with this action, there have been only three defaults (China in 1949, Cuba in 1961 and North Korea in 1974) in the postwar period. Thus, insufficient data prevent the estimator from using default in the strict sense of the word. The only exception to this is the largely theoretical paper by Eaton and Gersovitz (1981b), who equate default with outright repudiation. However, Eaton and Gersovitz do not attempt to estimate a probability of default. Rather, the objective of the study is to show that 'poor countries' are credit rationed on international capital markets because of the possibility of outright repudiation. Using this framework, Eaton and Gersovitz identify certain country characteristics relating to the demand and supply of sovereign loans. The objective of the Eaton and Gersovitz paper is quite different from the statistical studies that develop models designed to identify problem debtor countries.

The data problems arising from the use of outright repudiation have caused the statistical models to employ the rescheduling of sovereign external debt as a proxy for default on sovereign loans. However, this proxy is not without its own problems. A rescheduled sovereign loan is an agreement between borrower and lender to extend the maturity of the existing sovereign external debt. In this sense it represents a new loan agreement between borrower and lender. Consider for the moment the firm which manages to persuade its bankers to refinance its debt. There are very few of us who would classify this firm in the same group as those firms who repudiate their debt. Yet, because of insufficient data, this is exactly what is being done by researchers in the field of sovereign risk. There is nothing

wrong with using rescheduling cases in order to estimate the probability of rescheduling, provided no one is under the illusion that the
researcher is obtaining a satisfactory measure of the probability of
default. Yet, with the exception of Cline (1984), the literature does
give this impression. Nor is this just a problem of semantics. For the
lender, the outright repudiation of a debt represents a loss and is
recorded as such. Because rescheduling is a form of new loan agreement, it may not be a 'bad' event for the lender. This will depend upon
the net present value of the rescheduled loan compared with the
original loan. Preliminary research in this area (Heffernan *et al.*,
1985a) suggests that there have been cases where the percentage
change in the net present value of the loan has been positive, that is,
the loan has performed well by the net present value criterion. In other
cases, a net present value percentage loss was recorded. There were
several factors which explained the different performance on rescheduled sovereign debt, but this is not the place to discuss them. The
relevant point here is that the lender in fact can gain as a result of the rescheduling of sovereign debt. If this is true, we must ask the question:
what are the statistical models trying to predict? The term coined by
Taffler and Abassi (1984) may be useful in this respect: these are
really *early warning models*, signalling to the borrower and lender
alike that rescheduling may become necessary because of the country's
economic performance. Under no circumstances should they be
interpreted as indicators that a country is likely to repudiate its debt.

EXPLANATORY OR INDEPENDENT VARIABLES

The explanatory variables that are tested for statistical significance
vary from model to model. Taffler and Abassi (1984) have tested a
most extensive range of variables (42 in number) but other studies
confine their data base to a few variables. Below are listed most of the
variables that have been frequently tested for significance in the
published literature. Although this list is not exhaustive, it is representative. The variables can be placed in one of three categories:
current account variables, capital account variables, and 'other'
variables.

CURRENT ACCOUNT VARIABLES

1 The Debt-Service Ratio: (DSR) This is the ratio of external
debt-service payments to the value of exports of goods and services.
Normally, the researcher gathers data from the World Bank's *World
Debt Tables*, which reports annual levels of nominal external debt
owed by the country in question. The World Bank draws a distinction
between publicly guaranteed external debt, debt incurred through

official financing, and private external debt. The last two categories are excluded from the statistical studies of sovereign risk analysis. Although the data on long-term public debt are available for most developing countries, the World Bank does not distinguish between long-term and short-term debt. A recent publication by the Bank for International Settlements (BIS), *The Maturity Distribution of International Bank Lending*, does permit us to compute the percentage of total external debt that is short term, but only from 1977 onwards.

The correct terminology for the debt being referred to is *Nominal Sovereign* (or publicly guaranteed) *External Debt*. To simplify matters, this is referred to as external or sovereign debt for the remainder of this book.

The numerator of the DSR is made up of the service on the country's external debt. Debt-service refers to the payment of principal plus interest in a given year. In the studies, this consists of the gross interest payments on all external debt, plus the repayment of principal (amortization) on the medium-term and long-term debt.

The value of exports of goods and services appears in the denominator of the DSR. This information may be obtained for most countries from the IMF's *International Financial Statistics*, which is published on a monthly basis with an annual summary.

The DSR gives an indication of the size of foreign exchange earnings absorbed by the external debt-service payments of the country. We would expect a positive relationship between this explanatory variable and the dependent variable, the probability of rescheduling. The reasoning is straightforward: if a country experiences a sudden decline in foreign exchange earnings in relation to its debt-service burden or a sudden increase in the latter relative to a given level of foreign exchange earnings, the country could well be forced into rescheduling or even outright repudiation of its debt. Unfortunately there is no magic number (such as the 20 per cent frequently cited) that will tell the analyst the threshold at which a country could get into trouble. For example, during the 1930s, Canada and Australia had DSRs of 35 per cent and 40 per cent respectively; certain Latin American nations (Bolivia, Brazil, Colombia, Cuba, Peru and Uruguay) all had DSRs that were considerably lower than these, yet these countries defaulted on their bond repayments.

2 The Ratio of External Debt to the Value of Exports of Goods and Services: (D/EX) The denominator of this indicator is the same as that for the DSR, but the numerator consists of total external sovereign debt. Some researchers have used the ratio of net debt to exports of goods and services (the latter consists of gross external debt less non-gold reserves held at the country's central bank). The main difference between either of these two ratios and the DSR lies in the longer-term nature of the former. An annual DSR can act as an indicator of immediate problems, whereas the last two signal the long-term external commitments of a country, measuring as they do the country's total external debt in a given year as opposed to what must be serviced in the year. Either ratio (and especially the DSR) is easily distorted because they fail to identify the maturity structure of the debt, an important aspect of any country's ability to repay its external debt. For example, if a high proportion of the external debt matures at a certain future date, the implicit bunching of maturities would raise the DSR at that date, although it would be substantially lower at other dates.

Many of the statistical studies test both variables and find at least one to be statistically significant. Cline (1984) uses either the DSR or the ratio of net debt to exports in alternative tests and finds both are statistically significant. On the other hand, Taffler and Abassi (1984) find the ratio of external debt to exports significant, but the DSR does poorly. There does not seem to be a satisfactory explanation of why different studies find such a high variance of performance with respect to these variables.

3 Ratios of Imports to GNP (GDP) and Non-Compressible Imports to Total Imports: (IM/GNP or IM/GDP)   The ratio of 'non-compressible' imports to total imports of goods and services is an attempt to capture a measure of flexibility when it comes to cutting back on the import bill. Non-compressible imports are those imports that are 'necessities' to the economy, including certain foodstuffs, intermediate goods and capital goods. The higher the ratio the more difficult it would be to cut back on the import bill and, hence, the higher the probability of rescheduling. Unfortunately there are serious measurement problems with this variable. Data on the composition of imports vary in availability from country to country, and it is often difficult to draw the line between a necessary import and a luxury import.

Gross National Product (GNP) differs from Gross Domestic Product (GDP) in that the latter excludes economic activity conducted in the debtor country by non-resident entities. The information is available from a number of sources including the IMF's IFS publications.

The use of the ratio of imports to GNP (GDP) reflects an attempt to provide an indication of the degree to which national income growth will be affected should a country have to reduce its import bill in response to debt-servicing difficulties. The higher this ratio, the greater the likelihood of rescheduling, because the country is more likely to be dependent on imports to sustain production and hence economic growth. Ideally, we would want a ratio of intermediate goods imports to GNP but, again, there would be difficulties in measurement.

4 Ratio of International Reserves to the Import of Goods and Services: (RES/IM) This ratio is an indicator of short-term liquidity problems. Some researchers express it in terms of months, that is, the number of months for which reserves are available given the value of the country's import bill. Practitioners tend to think that an availability of reserves of less than three months is a danger signal. Again, it is difficult to generalize, because some countries have disproportionately high import bills at certain times of the year. Other studies use the percentage computed from the ratio where the higher the percentage of reserves in relation to imports, the more likely it is that reserves can be drawn upon should export revenues be unexpectedly low. Hence, the probability of rescheduling falls. Thus, we would expect a negative relationship between this variable and the dependent variable.

5 Growth Rate of Exports: (GEX) This variable is straight-forward. A country with a rapid growth rate of exports of goods and services is more likely to be earning the revenues required to service its debt. Hence, we would expect to find a negative relationship between this independent variable and the probability of rescheduling. To avoid the distortionary effects arising from changes in prices and cyclical fluctuations, the variable is expressed in real or volume terms and an average (based on a number of years) export growth rate is employed.

6 Variance in Export Earnings: (VAREX) Stable export earnings reduce the likelihood of a country's encountering debt-servicing difficulties, because the country is unlikely to experience sudden discrepancies in its balance of payments. Again, it is wise to take an average of the percentage deviation from trend over a number of years. The higher the variance, the higher is the probability of rescheduling.

7 The Ratio of the Current Account Deficit to the Export of Goods and Services: (CAX) This ratio is meant to provide an indication of the country's new borrowing requirements in a given year. In order to make different countries' deficits comparable, the current account deficit is divided by the country's export of goods and services.

CAPITAL ACCOUNT VARIABLES

1 The Ratio of Capital Inflows to Debt-Service: (K/DS)   Capital inflows in the form of direct investments, grants, transfer payments and new loans all contribute to the country's foreign exchange receipts, which in turn ease the servicing of external debt. Hence there is a negative relationship between this ratio and the probability of rescheduling: as capital inflows rise, the probability of rescheduling (at least in the short term) falls. At least one statistical model (Feder, Just and Ross, 1981) distinguishes between:

(a) the ratio of net non-commercial foreign exchange inflows to debt-service: the numerator includes capital grants, workers' remittances, net current transfers, and net medium-term and long-term loans from governments and international organizations;

(b) the ratio of commercial foreign exchange inflows to debt-service: the numerator is defined as medium-term and long-term loans granted by foreign commercial banks and direct investment net of repatriated direct investment income. The authors separate capital inflows in this way, because they argue that items under (b) are more flexible and do not tend to be tied to specifics the way items under category (a) are. In addition, the authors argue, if a large proportion of inflows are commitments by commercial banks, refinancing arrangements are more likely to be forthcoming. The study by Kharas (1984) uses capital inflows net of amortization (NFE) as a percentage of GDP. This numerator represents gross capital inflows less principal repayments in a given year.

2 The Ratio of Amortization to External Debt: (A/D)   This is probably the most controversial of all the explanatory variables employed in the statistical studies. It was first introduced by Frank and Cline (1971). These authors argued that the inverse of this ratio represented the average maturity of a country's external debt. A country with a high proportion of long-term average debt will prove to be highly inflexible should it (in the event of debt-servicing difficulties) be required to cut back on its external debt. Also, the low ratio could suggest the country was unable to negotiate short-term loans. Given this inflexibility, the probability of rescheduling will be greater the higher is the average maturity of debt or the lower the ratio.

There are several difficulties with the Frank and Cline interpretation of how this ratio influences the probability of a country rescheduling its sovereign loans. First, a high average maturity may not be the best proxy for the degree of flexibility in an economic system should it encounter difficulties servicing its debt. The most direct way of dealing with the problem is to reduce the import bill and raise export revenues. It is unlikely that a country would cut back on borrowing as anything but a secondary response. Secondly, there are data problems for countries which have rescheduled, because an estimate of amortization is required for the year of rescheduling. Finally, this variable and the debt-service ratio cannot be independent of each other, because amortization enters the numerators of both ratios. If both are used as explanatory variables (as they were with Frank and Cline, 1971) the statistical test will be plagued by problems of 'multicollinearity'. This arises whenever explanatory variables are thought to be independent of each other but are not. If present, it will be impossible to identify the relative importance of independent variables, and the estimates of the coefficients on the variables will be highly sensitive to particular sets of sample data. This is a serious deficiency in many of the statistical models and receives more attention later in this chapter (pp. 64–5).

Cline (1984) interprets this ratio differently. He argues that it represents the rate of amortization and is inversely related to the probability of rescheduling. Cline reasons that for a *given* DSR, a high rate of amortization will reduce the probability of rescheduling. Although this argument is more intuitively appealing than that made by Frank and Cline, it does depend on an unchanged DSR. If the DSR is rising simultaneously with amortization, the model will suffer from problems of multicollinearity.

3 Commitment per Capita: (C/POP) This is the ratio of new debt contracted during a given year to population. It is used in the Taffler and Abassi (1984) study as a proxy for wealth because it is highly correlated with per capita income and external debt per capita. This suggests that wealthier countries borrow more and, therefore, are less likely to reschedule.

OTHER VARIABLES
1 Ratio of International Reserves to External Debt: (RES/D)
International reserves are held at the central bank of the country and include foreign exchange reserves, reserve positions held with the IMF, the US dollar value of gold reserves and SDRs: the special drawing rights allocated to the country by the IMF. The data are available from the IMF's IFS. Some authors have excluded gold from

the calculation of reserves on the grounds that the fraction of gold in total reserves varies from country to country and this in turn raises the size of the random error in the variable (Cline, 1984, p. 213).

Expressed as a percentage of total outstanding external debt, this provides an indication of the country's international reserves that will be absorbed by its external commitments. In this sense it is a long-term indicator. As this ratio rises, the probability of rescheduling should decline.

2 Per capita income: (Y/GNP) Per capita income is an indicator of a country's living standards. The higher the per capita income, the greater will be the consumption of non-essential items. This makes for greater flexibility in the adjustment of consumption patterns, should this become necessary because of increasing debt-servicing problems. Countries with low or subsistence-level per capita incomes lack this flexibility and, therefore, are more likely to need to reschedule. One statistical study (Feder, Just and Ross, 1981) employs the ratio of real per capita GNP to US per capita GNP in order to emphasize the importance of the income-level of the country in question in relation to that of the United States.

3 Share of Investment in National Income: (I/GNP) This provides the analyst with an indicator of the importance placed on investment by the country: we would be looking for a steady annual rise in this ratio. Some models use the share of investment in total absorption, the latter being defined as GDP less imports plus exports. The higher the value of this ratio, the lower the probability of rescheduling.

4 Ratio of External Debt to GNP (or GDP): (D/GNP or D/GDP) Either of these ratios gives an indication of the external claim on a debtor country's current production. The ratio will be based on annual figures for numerator and denominator. The higher the ratio, the greater the likelihood that the country will need to reschedule.

5 Ratio of Reserves to GNP: (RES/GNP) Like the ratio of reserves to imports, this is an indicator of liquidity, because it gives the level of reserves in relation to the economy's current production. The higher the ratio, the lower the probability of rescheduling.

6 Monetary Indicators These indicators are an attempt to capture the effect of macroeconomic policy on the likelihood of rescheduling. The general belief is that countries following strict money supply growth targets are less likely to suffer from problems of domestic inflation, which would make them less competitive on world markets and hence prone to balance of payments problems. Most studies use the percentage change in the consumer price index (INF) as their indicator, though Taffler and Abassi (1984) also test domestic credit as a percentage of GDP (DC/GDP). It is worth stressing that these indicators are at best crude measures of an economy's overall macro-economic strategy.

7 World Credit Liquidity: (L)   One study (Cline, 1984) attempts to capture what should be an important supply side variable: the degree of credit abundance in the world economy. The more liquid the international credit markets, the less likely it is that rescheduling will be necessary. Unfortunately, the proxy used by Cline is not very satisfactory. He chooses the ratio of total net external borrowing by non oil developing countries to their total imports. The problem with this ratio lies in the numerator: it is difficult to conceive of it as being a sole indicator of supply. It could also rise because of a simultaneous increase in demand.

8 The Ratio of Domestic Savings to GNP: (S)   A country with a comparatively high savings ratio is less likely to reschedule because it is providing a domestic means by which the country's future economic growth may be financed. This will make the country less dependent on forms of external finance in future years.

9 Per Capita Rate of Economic Growth: (G)   This is similar to the per capita income measure, except that it is an indicator of how quickly per capita incomes are rising and, therefore, provides the analyst with a measure of the general health of the economy. If the growth rate declines, the country is likely to increase its borrowing in order to smooth consumption over time. This is part of the development cycle hypothesis discussed in Chapter 1. However, it is questionable whether the implied negative relationship between rescheduling and G follows from this hypothesis, since it will depend on the length of time the temporary drop in income growth rates lasts.

Sovereign Risk Analysis Using Discriminant or Logit Models

DISCRIMINANT ANALYSIS

Discriminant analysis is one of the statistical approaches applied to the analysis of sovereign risk. It begins from the premise that all quantifiable, pertinent data may be placed in two or more 'populations'. The term population is being used in the statistical sense: it means all the observations under consideration. The objective of discriminant analysis is to obtain a 'rule' (an estimated function), which will be able to assign an observation to a correct population.

When applied to sovereign risk analysis, it is assumed that a country can be assigned to one of two populations. The countries that re-schedule belong to one population (call this P_1) and countries which do not reschedule belong to the second population (P_2). The objective is to use data from past economic performance in order to derive a function that will discriminate between countries by placing them in one of the two populations. This function is called the *discriminant function*. There are three stages to the statistical exercise:

(1) Obtain a large enough sample of countries that fall into either of the two populations. Use the performance of economic variables for *all* the countries (the independent or explanatory variables) to construct a function that will discriminate between the two types of populations. Based on the economic information available for *each* country, this discriminant function is used to assign the country to one of the two populations.

(2) The discriminant function is constructed from 'in sample' obser-vations. Out of sample data should be employed to test the ability of the discriminant function to place a country in the correct population.

(3) Once satisfied that the function is not making too many errors, the model is used to predict countries that will or will not reschedule at some future date. This is an ex ante prediction by the model: it is using the discriminant rule to assign a country to a population in some future year. Only when this year has actually passed will the true predictive ability of the model become known.

More formally, define Z as a linear discriminant function of a number of independent, explanatory variables. Then:

$$Z = a_1 X_1 + a_2 X_2 + a_3 X_3 + \ldots + a_n X_n, \qquad i = 1, 2, \ldots, n$$

OR

$$Z = \sum_{i=1}^{n} a_i X_i$$

where

X_1 represents the independent explanatory variables. For example, most models test to see if the DSR has a statistically important influence on the probability of a country rescheduling.

a_i is the coefficient associated with the ith explanatory variable. If statistically significant, these coefficients will provide an indication of the relative importance of the economic variables to which they are attached.

The researcher begins by deciding which economic variables should be tested for statistical significance in relation to their ability to assign countries to one of the two populations. It is then necessary to gather data on these economic variables for a large enough sample of countries which fall into either of the two populations. Most of the studies focus their attention on developing nations (as defined in Chapter 1) because this is the only group which has a sufficiently large number of reschedulings to provide a reasonably good data base.

The developing countries are placed in one of the two populations: those that reschedule in a given year and those that do not. Combined with the information on rescheduling, the observations on the economic variables from all the countries are used to construct a rule: the researcher obtains a linear discriminant function Z and, associated with this estimated general function, the values for the coefficients attached to each economic variable found to be statistically significant.

Once the general discriminant function is obtained, the annual values of X_i for a given country are fed into the function and a 'Z score' is computed for the country in question. To use this Z score as a means of assigning a country to one of the two populations, it needs to be compared to a critical Z, $Z*$:

(1)   If a country has a Z score that is below $Z*$ ($Z < Z*$) the country is predicted to reschedule: it comes from P_1

(2)   If a country has a Z score that is greater than $Z*$ ($Z > Z*$) the country is predicted not to reschedule: it comes from P_2

There are two types of errors when it comes to the classification of countries. A Type I error is one where a country belonging to P_1 is classified in P_2, that is, the country reschedules when it is predicted not to reschedule. A Type II error occurs when a country is predicted to reschedule but does not, that is, the discriminant function assigns it to P_1 when it should be in P_2. Costs and probabilities are attached to these two types of errors to yield an expected cost function. The discriminant function and the critical value $Z*$ are jointly determined through an iterative procedure which minimizes the expected cost function.

Two published studies have employed the discriminant model to analyse sovereign risk. The Frank and Cline (1971) approach is reviewed in order to provide the reader with an illustration of the general principles of discriminant analysis outlined above. The data included 13 rescheduling cases in 8 countries and 132 non-reschedulings in 18 countries. The period of estimation was 1960–8. To estimate a general linear discriminant function, Frank and Cline tried eight economic (explanatory) variables:

1   The DSR
2   The growth rate of exports
3   Export variance
4   Non-compressible imports as a fraction of total imports
5   Per capita income
6   The ratio of debt amortization to total external debt
7   The ratio of imports to GNP
8   The ratio of imports to reserves

Having estimated the linear discriminant function using the iterative procedure mentioned earlier, Frank and Cline find that, of the eight economic variables, only three were both statistically significant and had the right sign. These were the DSR, M/RES, and A/D.

Taking the estimated discriminant function (Frank and Cline derived both linear and quadratic functions), the $Z*$, and the individual country values for the three ratios, a Z score is computed for each country and compared to $Z*$. From this it is possible to test the 'in sample' performance of the model through the number of Type I and II errors which occur. Frank and Cline wanted to find a 'best' linear function, i.e. a function which minimized the average number of errors. They found a two variable linear discriminant function with the DSR and A/D as the explanatory variables to be the 'best' function. With this function, there were 17 Type II errors and 1 Type I error, meaning the model erred on the cautious side. Of the 17 Type II errors, 13 were related to countries that did not reschedule in the year predicted but did reschedule in a nearby year. For example, the model predicted that Argentina would reschedule its external debt in 1962 and 1964, whereas the actual reschedulings took place in 1961 and 1963. The other 4 Type IIs were associated with Mexico.

Frank and Cline did use their final estimating equations to make predictions for future reschedulings. These are reserved for comparison with the predictive ability of other models to be found later in this chapter (pp. 54–5).

Taffler and Abassi (1984) also use a discriminant model to analyse sovereign risk. Data on developing countries from 1967 to 1977 were used to fit the discriminant function. Its performance was tested using out of sample data in 1978. Annual observations from 95 countries for 42 economic variables were collected. However, the final linear discriminant function contained only four explanatory variables that had the right sign and were statistically significant. These, along with the detail on the size of their sample, may be found in Table 2.3 (see p. 52). Of the four variables, the authors found that D/X and commitment per capita were more important as contributors to the model's performance than the other two 'monetary' variables: the inflation rate and the ratio of domestic credit to GDP. The commitment per capita variable is an indication of the country's ability to secure new loans on the international capital markets in a given year and, as such, may reflect the views of the international financial markets with respect to the country. It is the only study that finds such a variable statistically significant. The Type I and Type II errors associated with the in sample years are 10 per cent and 8.9 per cent of their respective populations. The ex ante predictive ability of the model was tested using a five-year period, 1979 to 1983. These results receive attention later in the chapter (see p. 56).

In an earlier version of their paper (1982), Taffler and Abassi transform the country Z scores into P scores. The Z scores of all the countries were ranked in ascending order. The P score gives the percentile where the country lies. It was obtained through the usual percentile calculation. For example, suppose a country's Z score ranks it as 75th out of 80 countries. Then the P score for this country will be:

$$P \text{ score} = 75/80 \times 100 = 93.75$$

To compare the P scores of different countries, it is necessary to compute a 'solvency threshold' P score. This is done by taking the critical Z score and transforming it into a percentile measure. For example, if the $Z*$ score is ranked 10th out of the 80 countries, the solvency threshold P score is 12.5. The P score permits the analyst to make cross-country comparisons, using the solvency threshold score as the basis for the comparison. In addition, the analyst can track the P scores of the countries over a number of years. A country with a P score that is falling over time and in danger of dropping below the threshold could be signalling future trouble.

LOGIT ANALYSIS

Like the use of discriminant analysis in SRA, the main objective is to employ a statistical technique to identify the economic variables that influence a country's probability of default/rescheduling.

The approach when using discriminant analysis assumed that countries came from one of two populations and, by using past observations on economic variables, a discriminant function was estimated. This permitted the analyst to identify the population to which a given country belonged, based on the values of its own economic variables.

The approach using logit analysis differs because it does not force countries into separate populations based on the values of certain economic variables. The logit approach assumes that the combined effect of certain economic variables will serve to push the country over a certain threshold – from being in the no rescheduling group to being in the rescheduling group or vice versa.

Logit analysis was developed to deal with cases of *BINARY* ('on'/'off') *EVENTS*, where the event is a *DEPENDENT* variable. Examples of the problem include using data to estimate the probability of purchase/no purchase decisions or the decision whether or not to take a certain degree course. In sovereign risk analysis the binary event is whether or not a country reschedules. There is no other classification for the country: either it reschedules or it does not. In the logit model, data are used to estimate this probability.

To further your understanding of the logit model, assume that the binary dependent variable is rescheduling and that the only independent variable influencing the probability of rescheduling is the ratio of external debt to exports (D/X). The relationship between D/X and the probability of rescheduling (PR) is generally accepted to be positive, i.e. an increase in D/X will raise PR. Figure 2.1 illustrates the logit model when there is only *one* independent variable, D/X. The D/X is on the horizontal axis and the PR on the vertical axis. The S-shaped curve is the logit transformation: when the value for the D/X is very low the probability of rescheduling is low, hence the relevant part of the curve is flat. It begins to get very steep as the D/X rises, and becomes horizontal at the upper end of the curve because the probability of default cannot exceed 1.

More generally, we can think of there being several independent variables which influence the probability of rescheduling, summarized by a vector z which would lie on the horizontal axis. Also, the horizontal axis need not be confined to positive numbers: the logit S can stretch from a negative part of the axis to the positive part. But the vertical axis must always be constrained to the part of the axis which lies between 0 and 1.

For a number of theoretical reasons which will not be discussed here, the logistic approach is favoured over the discriminant approach. But, in terms of ability to identify problem debtor countries, it appears that neither model has an advantage.[3]

A number of statistical studies of country risk have employed the logit model. These include Feder and Just (1977), Feder, Just and Ross (1981), Mayo and Barrett (1978) and Cline (1984). The main

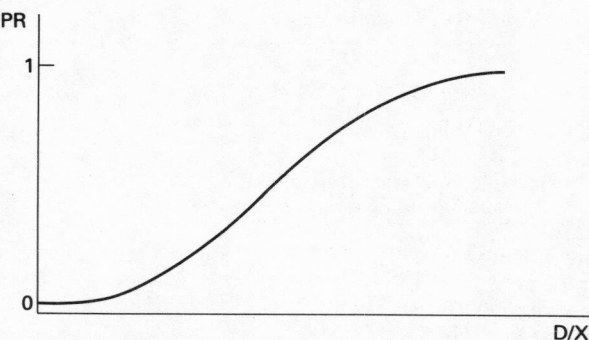

Figure 2.1 The logit transformation.

results of the studies will be given in Table 2.3 (p. 52). Below, the Cline study is examined in some detail to give the reader a further understanding of how a logit model works. Cline is chosen because, unlike all the other statistical investigations (using logit or discriminant analysis), Cline specifies both the supply and demand side of rescheduling. This makes his model more consistent with an economic approach to the problem.

Cline (1984, Appendix A) begins his logit analysis of the probability of rescheduling by identifying the variables that influence the supply of rescheduling, i.e. the lender's decision to enter into a rescheduling agreement, and the demand for rescheduling, the borrower's decision to reschedule the country's outstanding loans. On the demand side, Cline sets out to test some variables for statistical significance (see Table 2.1). On the supply side of rescheduling, the variables tested for statistical significance are given in Table 2.2.

Table 2.1 *Demand for Rescheduling*

Variable	(+) or (−) Influence on PR
Debt service ratio (DSR)	+
Foreign reserves/imports (RSM)	−
Per capita rate of economic growth (G)	−
Per capita income (Y)	−
Current account deficit/exports of goods and services (CAX)	−

While the influence of the independent variables on the demand side of Cline's model is straightforward, the expected signs of the variables

Table 2.2   *Supply of Rescheduling*

Variable	$(+) or (-)$ Influence on PR
Debt service ratio (DSR) OR	
Net debt*/export of goods and services (NDX)	+
Inflationary erosion of gross debt/export of goods and services (pD/X)	−
Amortization/debt (A)	−
Per capita income	−
Domestic savings/GNP (S)	−
Export growth rate (GEX)	−
World credit supply (L)	−

* Net debt = Gross debt − Reserves.

on the supply side require further elaboration. Cline believes the supply of rescheduling can be estimated by looking at the behaviour of the developed economies' supply curve of foreign credit, arguing that any variable that reduces the supply of foreign credit increases the probability that a disequilibrium will arise in the international credit markets because the foreign credit supply curve is being shifted to the left. This increased probability of a disequilibrium in turn raises the probability of rescheduling.

Let us examine the supply side variables in greater detail. Cline tests the DSR and the ratio of net debt to exports of goods and services as alternative variables, arguing that banks use these variables as part of their screening process when judging the economic viability of the country in question. The higher the value of these variables, the greater the likelihood that a country will be unable to meet its external obligations. This will have a negative impact on the supply of credit, raising the probability of rescheduling. There is a fundamental inconsistency in this argument: because it suggests bankers do not appear to realize that, by reducing their credit supply, the probability of a rescheduling problem rises. Further, as was argued earlier, we can think of rescheduling as representing a new loan agreement; hence, it is difficult to treat the supply of rescheduling as a strict consequence of the reduced supply of foreign credit. Although we can accept the idea that a lower supply will prompt a rescheduling, the rescheduling itself is a signal that supply has risen.

Another variable on the supply side of Cline's model is a debt erosion variable. As Cline correctly points out, to the extent that higher nominal interest rates reflect a higher rate of inflation, the country will be faced with higher debt service payments but it will also see the real value of its debt erode. Unfortunately, the former is immediate while the latter occurs with a lag. None the less, if lenders account for this in their assessment of the country, the more the debt is eroded by inflation, the more unlikely it is that a country will have to reschedule its loans. To proxy the inflation erosion of debt, Cline uses the world inflation rate multiplied by the total outstanding debt of the country. This is normalized by the country's exports of goods and services. The higher the degree of debt erosion the lower the probability of rescheduling.

The ratio of amortization to debt also enters the supply side of the model. Cline argues the supply of credit is more likely to be available the higher the rate of amortization (the ratio of amortization to debt) because, for a given DSR, total debt will be lower. Hence this variable and the probability of rescheduling are inversely related. This may be contrasted with the Frank and Cline (1971) use of this variable on the demand side of rescheduling. Using the same ratio as a proxy for the inverse of the average maturity of debt, Frank and Cline argued that the higher the ratio, the lower the probability of rescheduling, because the average maturity of debt was lower. The Cline (1984) argument is more intuitively appealing, but the argument only holds for an unchanged DSR. If debt service is rising simultaneously with the rate of amortization, it will be difficult to sort out the two influences. This is really the problem of multicollinearity (see p. 65).

The next three variables listed on the supply side table are easily understood. Like the variables already discussed they are used by the bank to assess the creditworthiness of the sovereign lender. If the country performs well in terms of these variables, it is unlikely to have to reschedule. The final variable, world credit supply, is quite different because it is not a country-specific variable. Rather, it will have an equal impact on the supply of rescheduling, independent of the country in question. In the Cline study, the proxy for world credit 'abundance' is the ratio of total net external borrowing by the NOLDCs to their total imports. Cline argues that this variable is inversely related to the probability of rescheduling, that is, an increase in the supply of international credit reduces the probability of rescheduling in all countries. Although the inclusion of such a variable is useful, it is questionable whether the proxy chosen is suitable. To see this, consider the increase in international credit which resulted from the OPEC price increases in 1974 and 1978 and the consequent increase in OPEC surpluses. Net borrowing by NOLDCs rose dramatically, and so did the import bill of net oil importers. It is difficult to interpret the latter two events as a proxy for the world credit supply because supply and demand were rising simultaneously.

Having reviewed the demand and supply sides of the Cline model it is possible to turn to his derivation of the final estimating equation using the logit approach. Cline estimates one reduced form equation for the probability of rescheduling, rather than separate equations for demand and supply. It is possible to estimate one reduced form version of the equation without worrying about simultaneity problems (which arise whenever the same variable influences demand and supply), because the variables that are common to both the demand and supply sides of the Cline model influence the probability of rescheduling in the same direction. However, the one equation approach does prevent identification of the relative importance of demand and supply when a variable influences both.

The reduced form equation estimated by Cline is:

$$z = b_1 \text{DSR*} + b_2 \text{RSM*} + b_3 \text{G} + b_4 \text{Y} + b_5 [h(\text{CAX})^2*] + b_7 (\text{pD*/X*})$$
$$+ b_8 \text{A*} + b_9 \text{S*} + b_{10} \text{GEX} + b_{11} \text{L}$$

where

$b_i, i = 1, \ldots, 11$ are the coefficients associated with each independent variable.

* indicates that the data are from the previous year; otherwise they are for the current year.

CAX: This variable is expressed in quadratic form to capture the idea that the effect of CAX on the demand for rescheduling is non-linear because current account deficits can usually increase over a fairly wide range without having any impact on the probability of rescheduling, but, at some critical point, it begins to have a dramatic influence.

DSR*: Cline also estimates an equation replacing DSR* with NDX*. The latter has the coefficient b_6.

Using the logit method, the above equation is estimated using maximum likelihood techniques. The resulting dependent variable, z, is then transformed into an indicator of the probability of rescheduling via the logit transform:

$$\text{PR} = 1/[1 + e^{-z}]$$

where e is the base of the natural logarithm. PR can vary from 0 to 1 depending on the value of z.

Once the estimates for the independent economic variables are made, a value for z has been obtained and the logit transform is complete, it is necessary to choose a critical value for PR, call this PR*. For PR > PR* the country is predicted to reschedule and for PR < PR* the country is considered credit worthy. Unlike the discriminant models where the critical $Z*$ was jointly determined with the discriminant function through an iterative procedure, the choice of PR* is somewhat arbitrary, left as it is to the estimator. As Cline points out, a choice of PR* = 0.5 is not very satisfactory because it would result in a very unbalanced distribution of errors: there would be a large number of Type I errors (a country not predicted to reschedule does) but only a very small percentage of Type II errors (a country predicted to reschedule does not). To deal with this problem, the Cline study chooses the PR* which minimizes the total error, subject to the constraint that there is an equal error percentage rate in the two classes of observations. Note that it is possible to vary the weights attached to the error percentage rates. For example, highly risk averse lenders who are very concerned about Type I errors could place a heavier weight on this type of error, in which case the critical threshold, PR*, would be lower than in the case where the error rate in the two classes was given an equal weight.

The Cline model has been used in order to demonstrate the main principles of logit analysis as it applies to the credit assessment of sovereign borrowers. The results of this study, together with the findings of the other major statistical models (discriminant and logit) in this field, are summarized in Table 2.3 (see p. 52).

DISCUSSION OF TABLE 2.3

All of the statistical models were developed with the objective of predicting problem debtor countries. Before looking at their performance in greater detail, it is worth commenting on some of the individual aspects of the studies cited in Table 2.3, which have not received any attention up to this point.

The studies by Feder and Just (1977), Feder, Just and Ross (1981), Mayo and Barrett (1978), and Cline (1984) employed the logit approach in the derivation of an estimating equation. Hence these analysts had to assign a value to PR*, the critical threshold level for PR, the probability of rescheduling. Consequently, the number of Type I errors varies directly (and Type II errors inversely) with the value given to PR*. The lower the PR* the higher the number of Type II errors and the lower the number of Type I errors, i.e. the models will tend to err more on the cautious side. Feder and Just found that no matter what the PR* (0.1 to 0.9) there were no more than 11 errors. At PR* = 0.4, there were three Type I errors and 6 Type II errors.[4] In the study by Feder, Just and Ross, there were 20 Type I errors and 6

Table 2.3   *Summary of Statistical Models*

Model	Explanatory variables[1]	Data/Estimating years
Frank and Cline (1971)	DSR, A	17 LDCs; RS: 13 in 8 countries; non-RS: 132 in 18 countries; Discriminant Model, 1960–8
Feder and Just (1977)	DSR, M/RES, Y, K/DS	41 LDCs; RS: 21 in 11 countries; non-RS: 217; Logit Model, 1965–72
Mayo and Barrett (1978)	D/X, RES/M, M/GDP, IMFRES/M, INF	48 LDCs; RS (5 years): 28 in 11 countries; Logit Model, 1960–75
Feder, Just and Ross (1981)	DSR, y/USy, RES/M, X/GNP, non-COMMINF/DS, COMMINF/DS	580 observations; RS: 40; Logit Model, 1965–76
Taffler and Abassi (1984)	D/X, C/POP, INF, DC/GDP	95 LDCs; RS: 55 in 11 countries; non-RS: 660; Discriminant Model, 1967–77
Cline (1984)	DSR or D/X, M/RES, A, CAX, growth rate of Y, L	60 countries (mainly LDCs); RS: 22 in 15 countries; 670 observations; Logit Model, 1968–82
Kharas (1984)	DS/GDP, NFE/GDP, POP/GDP, I/GDP	43 countries; RS: 30 in 11 countries; 441 observations; Probit Model*, 1965–76.

Notes and abbreviations for Table 2.3 (in order of appearance)

[1]These are the explanatory variables that were found to be statistically significant and included in the final estimating equation of the model.

DSR: Debt service ratio
A: Amortization/External debt
M/RES: Imports of goods and services/Reserves
Y: Income per capita
K/DS: Capital inflow/Debt service
D/X: External debt/Exports of goods and services
M/GDP: Imports/Gross Domestic Product
IMFRES/M: IMF Reserve Position/Imports
INF: % Change in the Consumer Price Index
y/USy: Real per capita GNP/US real per capita GNP
non-COMMINF/DS: non-commercial inflows/Debt service
COMMINF/DS: Commercial inflows/Debt service
C/POP: Commitment per capita
DC/GDP: Domestic credit/GDP

Type II errors at PR* = 0.2. The likelihood ratio index (analogous to R^2 in linear regression) for these two studies were, respectively, 0.9 and 0.85.[5]

The model developed by Mayo and Barrett is slightly different in that it was designed to predict rescheduling up to five years in advance. The paper does not report the errors that accompany the final estimating equation. It does report a log likelihood ratio index of 0.63, implying an overall accuracy rate of 63 per cent. The Cline study reports that PR* = 0.041 is the critical threshold at which the model minimizes total error, subject to the constraint that the errors be balanced across the two classes of distribution. Compared with other studies, this threshold is considerably lower. Cline suggests that the low value is explained by the unbalanced sample in terms of the number of rescheduling cases. Of 670 country year observations, rescheduling cases make up only 3 per cent of the sample. In the 'best' model estimated by Cline, 9.1 per cent of the rescheduling cases are Type I errors and 13 per cent of the non-rescheduling cases are Type II errors. The log likelihood ratio is not reported, but Cline does state that the best model is accurate in 85 per cent of the rescheduling and non-rescheduling cases (Cline, 1984, p. 221).

In the paper by Kharas (1984), a probit model is employed in order to assess the probability of a country becoming uncreditworthy, as proxied by the need to reschedule. Probit analysis uses a methodology similar to logit analysis and, for the purposes of this text, requires no further explanation. The data base was somewhat limited, covering the period 1965 to 1976 for 43 countries. This involved 30 reschedulings in 11 countries. At a critical threshold of 0.125, it was found that 7 per cent of the predicted reschedulings were Type II errors (29 cases) and 17 per cent of the non-rescheduling predictions were Type I errors (5 cases). Note that these predictions were based on in sample data.

CAX: Current account deficit/Exports

L: Global credit abundance as proxied by the ratio of net external borrowing of NOLDCs to total imports of these countries

NFE/GDP: capital inflows net of amortization/GDP

I/GDP: Investment/GDP

LDCs: Lesser developed countries

RS: Rescheduling – all the models included RS by a country on an annual basis except for Mayo and Barrett who looked at RS over a five-year period.

non-RS: non-rescheduling

*The probit model, like the logit model, is for binary dependent variables. The estimating technique is similar to that of logit.

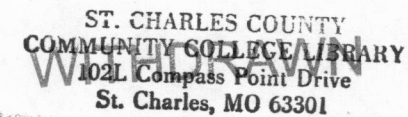

Predictive Ability of the Statistical Models

The performance of a model of sovereign risk analysis is best measured by examining its predictive ability. This section seeks to answer two related questions:

(1) How many Type I and Type II errors arise when the model is used to predict reschedulings beyond the country years included in the sample?

(2) Do the rankings produced by the *Institutional Investor*'s qualitative approach bear any relation to the ranking of countries produced by a statistical model?

Begin by examining the predictive ability of the statistical models cited in Table 2.3. Frank and Cline (1971) use their two variable linear discriminant functions to predict the debt-servicing capacity of 17 LDCs. The authors made projections of total sovereign external debt, interest payments, amortization payments, and the DSRs for the period 1967 to 1992. The DSR was computed on the basis of three different assumptions about export growth rates: a continuation of the 1960 to 1967 trend rate of growth for each country, a 4 per cent rate of export growth and an 8 per cent growth rate. The data sources were the World Bank's projections of the debt-service payments due in the period 1967 to 1992, given the level of debt outstanding in 1967. Frank and Cline did not attempt to predict the actual year of rescheduling. Rather they computed the percentage of country years when a country was likely to encounter debt-servicing difficulties in the period 1967 to 1992. From these projections, the authors classified the countries into one of three groups:

Group I: Independent of export growth rates, these countries were predicted to encounter serious debt-servicing difficulties. That is, for the period 1968 to 1992 the percentage of country years for which these countries are likely to get into trouble is close to 100. The group included India, Indonesia, Pakistan and Tunisia. All of these countries have since rescheduled their debts, with the exception of Tunisia.

Group II: Countries in this group were predicted to reschedule if export growth rates were low and capital imports continued on an upward trend. The countries were: Brazil, Chile, Colombia, The Dominican Republic, Israel, South Korea, Peru and Turkey. South Korea and Israel have not rescheduled their debts and Turkey did not reschedule its debt until after 1978. Brazil, after rescheduling in 1961 and 1964, did not reschedule again until 1983.

Group III: This group was predicted not to encounter debt-servicing difficulties under any conditions. In this category are some familiar names: Argentina, Mexico, Nigeria, Bolivia and Iran. All but Iran have rescheduled their debts. That is, four of the five predictions are Type I errors. Of this group, Argentina has rescheduled the most often: in 1962, 1965 and 1983.

As an educational tool, these rather dated predictions are useful. Of special note are its Type I errors, which arise because of the group III classification. It is instructive to point out what the model missed. First, the predictions were based on the World Bank's projection of debt service as reported in the *World Debt Tables*. The author has not come across a World Bank publication that actually explains how these projections are made. However, an examination of the figures reveal that they have systematically underestimated the debt-service obligations for most of the countries reported. Secondly, the average annual export growth rates in many of the newly industrializing countries were well above the maximum predicted rate of 8 per cent. South Korea and Brazil are notable examples of very high average annual growth rates. Finally, the model missed out on a number of critical random shocks (discussed in Chapter 1), which had serious balance of payments implications. These included the sharp rise in real rates of interest after 1978, the oil price shocks (which had a direct impact on oil importing LDCs), world recession, and the subsequent decline in the LDCs' terms of trade. Since the final estimating equation focused exclusively on two economic variables, most of the impact of the shocks was missed. By definition, no forecaster can predict random shocks, but they do occur in the world economy and models that ignore them are bound to have a large number of errors.

Kharas (1984) claims to incorporate random shocks into a theoretical-cum-empirical model of long-run creditworthiness. However, having derived an estimating equation, the author makes no attempt to predict reschedulings. There are also some problematic points in the Kharas model. Kharas suggests that a negative random shock, which reduces the capital stock below some critical level, will always result in the country losing its creditworthiness on international capital markets. Kharas also equates rescheduling with a loss of creditworthiness. Further, in the final estimating equations there is no provision for a random shock parameter despite the emphasis placed on this in the theoretical part of the paper. Kharas excepted, the lack of attention paid to the issue of random shocks is a serious omission in these models, a problem which is addressed in Chapter 3.

The empirical studies by Feder and Just (1977), Feder, Just and

Ross (1981) and Mayo and Barrett (1978) are rather weak when it comes to testing the predictive abilities of their models. Feder and Just (1977) use an indirect test. Recall that the estimation period for their model was 1965 to 1972. Using the data on the variables found to be statistically significant, Feder and Just compute the default probability predictions for the countries that borrowed on the Eurodollar market in the period 1973–4. Of this group, eight loans associated with three countries had predicted default probabilities that were greater than 0.12 (above the default threshold). Feder and Just report that three of the loans in this category are associated with a country reported to be seeking a rescheduling agreement. The indirect method used to test the model's performance and the small sample size prevent us from being able to judge this model's predictive ability. In the paper by Feder, Just and Ross (1981) no predictions are made. Performance is judged by an out of sample test of the model, using data for the period 1977–9. A total of 135 observations were collected for this period, 10 of these relating to countries which had rescheduled or requested rescheduling. They find that compared to the in sample base, the number of Type I errors does not change and Type II errors rise slightly. The authors conclude that there has been little change in the explanatory power of the model when out of sample data are used (p. 664). However, as in the earlier study, the sample size is relatively small. Also there is no true test of the ex ante predictive ability of the model.

Mayo and Barrett (1978) defined their rescheduling group to include reschedulings up to five years later. This is in contrast to the other models, where rescheduling was identified for one year forward. The paper does not report the error rates associated with the in sample model nor does it attempt any ex ante predictions.

In terms of testing predictive ability the work by Taffler and Abassi (1984) is the most comprehensive of all the published papers. Using the formal rescheduling cases which took place from the beginning of 1979 to the end of 1983, the performance of the model is measured in terms of its predictive ability over this period. A country with a negative Z score in the year t is predicted to reschedule in the year $t + 1$. During this period, 71 rescheduling cases were identified, with 63 per cent of these occurring during 1983. The model correctly predicted 50 of these cases or 69 per cent of the sample. The number of Type I errors ranged from a minimum of 2 in 1980 to a maximum of 7 in 1982. Several countries appeared as Type I errors more than once: Ecuador, Venezuela, Liberia, Senegal and Guyana. Taffler and Abassi admit that this may reflect a weakness in their model when it is used to predict the performance of single commodity (including oil) based producers and countries where the data sources are either weak or unreliable.

In the five-year period, there was a total of 83 Type II errors. The number of Type II errors ranged from a minimum of 15 in 1981 and 1982 to a maximum of 20 in 1983. Three types of countries can be identified among these Type II errors. First, 38 of the cases were countries that are highly dependent on foreign aid and concessional lending. Another 21 cases were countries where rescheduling has been effectively postponed because of their access to new loans during this period. This group includes Brazil and Argentina, both of which rescheduled in 1984. Finally, four of the 83 Type II errors were characterized by political instability during this period.

Heffernan *et al.* (1983) compare the Taffler–Abassi *P* score rankings with the annual country rankings issued by the *Institutional Investor* (II). Designating the Taffler and Abassi model as a quantitative approach and the II survey results as a qualitative approach, it is an interesting exercise to test for the degree of correlation in country ranking produced by the two models. Confidence in country rating techniques would be enhanced if a high degree of correlation were found. To facilitate comparison, only the countries common to both models were included. In addition, the II rankings were translated into an *I* score by the following method:

$$I \text{ score} = 1/N \, (N - \text{II rank})$$

where N is the number of countries common to both models and the II rank is the renumbered II rank among the common countries. The I score is directly comparable with the Taffler–Abassi P score. Heffernan *et al.* tested for the degree of association between the two scores by computing a Spearman rank correlation coefficient, r.[6] The two systems would be perfectly positive correlated if r were found to be unity. On the other hand, if r is found to be close to zero, we would conclude that there is little association. In terms of a graph, if we put the I rank on the horizontal axis and the P rank on the vertical axis and plotted the associated country rankings, a perfect positive correlation would produce a positively sloped 45° line (see Figure 2.2).

Looking at the annual rankings for the period 1979 to 1982, the study found a positive but weak relationship between the two systems, with r ranging from 0.393 in 1981 to 0.517 in 1982. Dividing the rankings into two geographical regions, Africa and Latin America, the authors found a closer positive correlation for Africa ($r = 0.736$) than for Latin America ($r = 0.162$). The better performance for the African region is explained by the near perfect correlation for certain African nations, including Nigeria, Tunisia, the Ivory Coast, the Cameroons,

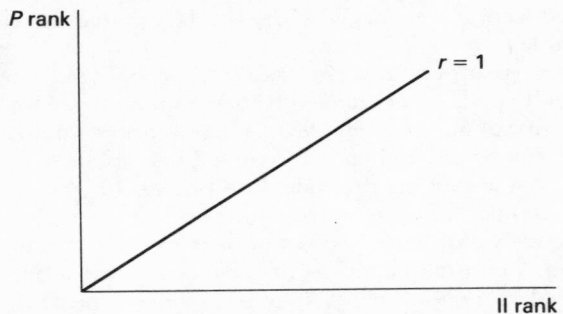

Figure 2.2   A perfect, positive correlation between the *P* and II ranks.

Senegal, Sudan, Zaire and Uganda. Otherwise there is little or no association. These findings are indicative of large discrepancies in the two ranking systems, a cause for concern for all practising analysts.

The study by Heffernan *et al*. went one step further and compared the predictive ability of the Taffler–Abassi study with that of the II. It should be stressed that the *Institutional Investor* does not claim to provide a prediction service from its country rankings. However, we would expect that countries with a high II rank would be most likely to encounter debt-servicing difficulties and that those with a low rank would not. To test this hypothesis, the 1981 II rank for countries (horizontal axis) was plotted against the rescheduling status of the country in 1982 (vertical axis), with each country being assigned a value of 1 if it did not reschedule and 0 if it did reschedule. Ideally one would observe a bunching of countries as shown in Figure 2.3. The actual plot (see Table 2.4) indicates that, with the exception of two Latin American countries (Peru and Argentina), the II correctly assigned a high rank to countries that rescheduled. But the spread of countries across the horizontal axis from point 1 on the vertical axis suggests that the model does err on the cautious side for many of the countries.

Taffler and Abassi (1984) attempt a similar comparison of predictive ability. In this case, an II default threshold was determined by using the II credit rating for 1980 and 1981 in conjunction with rescheduling cases for 1980 and 1981. This was then applied to the 1981 and 1982 rankings to predict cases of rescheduling in 1982 and 1983. Looking at countries common to both models, these II 'predictions' were compared with those made by the Tafler and Abassi model. The discriminant approach yielded a correct prediction rate of 71 per cent compared with 63 per cent for the II. The reschedulings

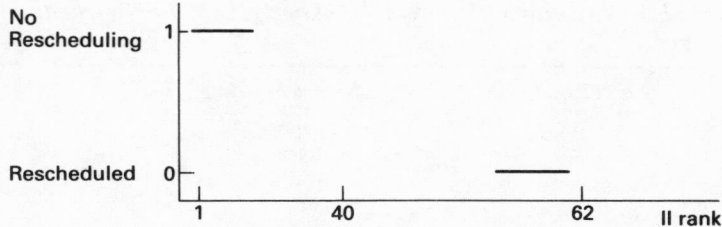

Figure 2.3 II-ranked countries, classified by rescheduling status.

by Mexico, Nigeria and Venezuela were not predicted by either approach. The II model missed some of the Latin American reschedulings predicted by the Taffler Abassi model, namely, Argentina, Brazil, Costa Rica and Chile. Finally, the II model correctly placed Liberia in two out of three years, a country which was a Type I error in the discriminant model.

Cline (1984) develops a full-fledged debt projection model in order to predict future problem countries. Cline makes a number of alternative assumptions about the future values of a number of economic variables. These are inserted into the logit model described in the last section, enabling Cline to make projections about the probability of rescheduling in 19 of the largest debtor countries for each year up to 1986. As was noted earlier, the Cline projections are based on an unconstrained balance of payments model, i.e. with no specified finance constraint. Cline determines the future indebtedness of the country by looking at the growth in net current account deficits: deficits less direct investment (this is a capital flow that does not create new debt) and drawdown of reserves.

The alternative assumptions on economic variables relate to world economic conditions expected to prevail up to 1986. Below, we cite Cline's 'base case' assumptions for four economic variables:

(1)   The OECD (Organization for Economic Cooperation and Development) growth rate is set at 3 per cent per annum for the period 1984 to 1986 and is assumed to be 1.5 per cent for 1983.

(2)   LIBOR (the London Interbank Offered Rate) gradually falls over the period:

1982: 15 per cent
1983: 10 per cent
1984: 9 per cent
1985: 8 per cent
1986: 8 per cent

Table 2.4   *Institutional Investor Rankings (1981) and Reschedulings (1982)*

	Rescheduling 0	No rescheduling 1
1		Singapore
2		Malaysia
3		Taiwan
4		Spain
5		Venezuela
6		Mexico
7		Greece
8		South Korea
9		Indonesia
10		Portugal
11		Algeria
12		Colombia
13		Trinidad and Tobago
14		Nigeria
15		Chile
16		Thailand
17	Argentina	
18		Brazil
19		Ecuador
20		India
21		Tunisia
22		Paraguay
23		Papua New Guinea
24		
25		Panama
26		Yugoslavia
27		Philippines
28		Uruguay
29		Ivory Coast
30		Jordan
31	Peru	Israel
32		Kenya
33		Gabon
34		Egypt
35		Cyprus
36		Morocco
37		Cameroon
38		Zimbabwe
39		Syria
40		Dominican Republic
41	Pakistan	
42	Malawi and Senegal	

Table 2.4 *Institutional Investor Rankings (1981) and Reschedulings (1982) (continued)*

	Rescheduling 0	No rescheduling 1
43		
44	Costa Rica	
45		Mauritius
46		Guatemala
47	Honduras	
48	Turkey	
49		Jamaica
50	Bolivia	
51		Congo
52	Liberia	
53		Zambia
54		Tanzania
55	Sierra Leone	
56		Iran
57	Sudan	
58		Ethiopia
59	Nicaragua	
60		El Salvador
61	Zaire	
62	Uganda	
I rank		

Cline also assumes that for all sovereign debt contracted at a variable rate of interest, the spread over LIBOR will be 1.5 per cent, except for Brazil where it will be 2 per cent.

(3) The dollar per barrel world price of oil is assumed to be $34.00 for 1982, dropping to $29.00 for the period 1983 to 1985 and rising to $34.00 in 1986.

(4) The real value of the dollar in relation to other major currencies is assumed to depreciate by 15 per cent over two years, beginning in 1984.

It should be noted that, in the projection model, the positive impact of OECD growth rates on the debt burden are substantially greater than the negative impact of higher LIBOR: Cline estimates that a '1 per cent rise in OECD growth rates has an impact on the debt burden equivalent to a 5 per cent reduction in LIBOR' (Cline, 1984, p. 60). He arrives at this estimate via the following reasoning. First, an increase in OECD growth rates of 1 per cent raises debtor-country export revenues by 6 per cent, a 3 per cent rise in volume and a 3 per cent rise in price. For NOLDCs, net external debt is on average 1.87 times the export of goods and services. Assuming two-thirds of the debt is indexed to LIBOR, a 1 per cent reduction in LIBOR cuts interest payments by 1.2 per cent (2/3 × 1.87), which in turn alleviates the debt burden. Thus, a 1 per cent increase in OECD growth rates would have an impact on the debt burden equivalent to a 5 per cent (6% ÷ 1.2) reduction in LIBOR. This figure varies from country to country, depending on whether it is an oil exporting developing nation (oil does not respond to higher OECD growth rates) and, also, on the size of its debt burden relative to exports. For example, the equivalent impact on the debt burden for Mexico is only 2.7 per cent because of its oil exporting status and its relatively high debt burden.

In addition to these external influences, Cline also allows for developing country domestic policies with respect to their growth rates and exchange rates. But they do not receive the close attention given to the external factors. Also, Cline divides the developing nations into NOLDCs and oil exporting developing nations. Cline's non oil developing country classification is different from the one employed by the IMF. For example, Cline has an OPEC grouping which is made up of developing countries not in capital surplus: Algeria, Ecuador, Nigeria, Indonesia and Venezuela. In the IMF classifications all of these countries (with the exception of Ecuador) are grouped as oil exporting nations. In addition, it should be noted that the 19 countries include eastern European debtors.

These assumptions were fed into Cline's logit model, which yielded predictions of rescheduling to 1986 (see Table 2.5). The table indicates five problem countries for which PR scores are above that of the critical threshold level. These are Brazil (to 1985), Mexico (to 1984), Argentina (to 1984), Chile (to 1984) and Ecuador (to 1986). Hence the outlook is fairly bright if the Cline predictions are accepted. However, a number of points should be made about the underlying assumptions. First, the debt burden is highly responsive to OECD growth rates: Cline himself admits that the severity of the problem recedes only for a sustained OECD growth rate of approximately 3 per cent per annum. In the 'worst case' scenario where growth rates are equal to an average annual growth of 1.4 per cent, Cline anticipates serious debt-servicing difficulties. World recession could push debtor countries into yet another round of refinancing. Cline wisely confines his predictions to the period to 1986. However, this is when the grace

Table 2.5   *Cline's (1984) Debt-Management Predictions. Projections of Logit Indicator of Debt-Servicing Difficulties in Nineteen Major Debtor Countries, 1980–6.*

	1980	1981	1982	1983	1984	1985	1986
Brazil	0.026	0.747	0.810	0.999	0.909	0.402	0.144
Mexico	0.135	0.021	0.435	0.949	0.679	0.241	0.129
Argentina	0.000	0.002	0.311	0.691	0.730	0.121	0.026
Korea	0.027	0.004	0.027	0.004	0.002	0.001	0.001
Venezuela	0.000	0.000	0.000	0.000	0.000	0.000	0.001
Philippines	0.002	0.001	0.050	0.265	0.406	0.133	0.073
Indonesia	0.000	0.000	0.001	0.015	0.010	0.008	0.011
Israel	0.003	0.004	0.033	0.018	0.056	0.042	0.063
Turkey	n.a.	n.a.	0.542	0.189	0.189	0.066	0.031
Yugoslavia	0.009	0.007	n.a.	0.074	0.041	0.011	0.005
Chile	0.000	0.000	0.265	0.650	0.369	0.105	0.051
Egypt	0.049	0.009	0.197	0.604	0.467	0.202	0.148
Algeria	0.003	0.001	n.a.	0.178	0.050	0.109	0.322
Portugal	0.002	0.016	0.164	0.447	0.263	0.073	0.036
Peru	n.a.	0.000	n.a.	0.095	0.220	0.094	0.074
Thailand	0.001	0.001	0.024	0.021	0.011	0.003	0.002
Romania	0.018	0.020	0.054	0.015	0.006	0.002	0.001
Hungary	n.a.	n.a.	n.a.	0.012	0.005	0.002	0.001
Ecuador	0.000	0.000	0.051	0.788	0.669	0.459	0.483

Note: The critical threshold level, PR*, is 0.242.
Source: Cline (1984), Table 3.9, p. 65.

periods associated with many of the 1983–4 rescheduling agreements begin to expire. Combined with a slowdown in OECD growth rates, the end of the grace periods could well provoke a refinancing crisis.

Secondly, Cline's assumptions about future values of LIBOR seem to be underestimates, while the price of oil is overestimated. The continued strength of the dollar also calls into question the Cline estimates. Indeed, part of Cline's 'worst case' scenario assumptions includes an average LIBOR of 13.5 per cent and dollar depreciation of only 5 per cent. Only the current OECD growth rates are close to the 'base case' assumptions. If these change, then, by Cline's predictions, it may not be possible to manage the external debt of these countries.

Finally, as Suttle (1985) notes, the Cline model does not attempt to introduce the effect of cyclical activity in the world economy, even though he acknowledges the importance of random shocks. For example, the predictions are based on average annual growth rates but the *variance* of world income growth rates are crucial to the ability of a country to earn export revenues and so service the debt. Also, the supply side of the international capital markets are largely ignored.

There have been other projections on external debt manageability, but this section has been confined to reviewing the predictions that accompany the statistical models of sovereign risk analysis. For a recent critical review of the debt projection models, see Suttle (1985). Having surveyed the standard approaches to sovereign risk analysis, this part of the chapter is concluded with a summary critique of the models.

Summary Critique of the Statistical Approaches to Sovereign Risk Analysis

The statistical models of sovereign risk have received an extensive review in this chapter. At several points a number of problems were cited. It is important to summarize these difficulties in order to stress to the reader the limitations of these models.

The first problem relates to the use of rescheduling as a proxy for default on external debt by a sovereign borrower. The implicit assumption is that rescheduling is a bad event for the lender. However, preliminary research by the author (Heffernan *et al.*, 1985a) suggests that this may not be the case for many of the rescheduling cases undertaken in the 1980s. If performance of the sovereign loan is measured by the percentage change in the net present value of the loan between the time of the original loan and the time it has rescheduled, then the research suggests that, at even reasonably high discount rates, the lenders may still have experienced a net present value percentage gain. This throws into doubt the purpose of the statistical studies that attempt to identify the variables crucial to rescheduling as if the event would prove to be an unprofitable one for the lender. Outright repudiation is always unprofitable, but can the same be said for rescheduling?

Secondly, the implied direction of causality in the models runs from the explanatory variables (such as the DSR) to the probability of rescheduling. However, the causality is highly likely to run in both directions. To see this, suppose that a lender perceives an increase in the probability of rescheduling or outright repudiation. His response may be to cut back on existing commitments in the country. This could in turn raise the likelihood of the country's having to reschedule or default. This is a problem that could be resolved through methods of simultaneous estimation, but the models would have to be extensively reworked before this is possible.

Thirdly, the author suspects the models suffer from serious problems of multicollinearity. Referring to column 2 of Table 2.3, we really have to question whether many of the explanatory variables found to be statistically significant in a given study are in fact independent of each other. Three of the studies find the DSR and capital inflows to debt service ratio to be statistically significant. Yet an increase in capital inflows could well affect the ability of the country to service its debt and, therefore, the DSR. It is questionable whether these ratios are truly independent of one another. The only paper reviewed which plays close attention to the problem of multicollinearity is the one by Taffler and Abassi (1984). These authors employ a varimax rotation method (1984, p. 548) in order to eliminate multicollinearity. Yet the final estimating equation includes the inflation rate and the ratio of domestic credit to GDP. It is hard to imagine that these variables are independent in a world with inflation expectations. In this case, a round of sustained inflation will increase the velocity of circulation of broadly defined money as a percentage of national income. This must in turn lower the ratio of DC to GDP. One wonders whether the varimax rotation is indeed removing all the multicollinearity.

This lack of independence between the so-called independent variables means it will not be possible to identify the relative importance of the different explanatory variables. More seriously, the variables are highly sensitive to particular sets of sample data. This may explain why such a wide variety of variables are identified in the studies as being statistically significant even though the years, statistical methodology and data sets overlap considerably.

All of these criticisms point to a more fundamental problem with these statistical models. By attempting to estimate a probability of default or rescheduling based on a number of economic variables, they are putting the cart before the horse. They provide no underlying framework of the supply and demand for sovereign loans. Yet this must be crucial to any explanation of why there is international sovereign borrowing and lending and, consequently, of why rescheduling or outright repudiation occur. It is really important to look at sovereign risk analysis by asking some fundamental questions about the supply and demand for sovereign loans. With no underlying framework of this sort, it is not surprising the statistical models have proved so problematic.

How International Banks Assess Country Risk

In this section, the question of how international banks are assessing country risk is reviewed by reference to a recent survey of 122 international banks, undertaken in London in August 1984 (Heffernan *et al.*, 1985b). The term, country risk, applies here because the survey included questions on bank attitudes to sociopolitical factors.

This survey differed from three related studies (Goodman, 1978; Mathis and Maslin, 1981; Burton and Inoue, 1983) in its objectives and/or its scope. The Goodman EXIM bank survey covered 37 banks, which accounted for half the international loans made by the US banking system. Through correspondence and personal interviews, Burton and Inoue surveyed 25 banks in 1980, eleven of which were based in the United States. The paper by Mathis and Maslin analysed a survey of 100 of the largest US banks conducted by Robert Morris Associates in June 1980. But the objective of this survey was to discover the methods by which banks measure country exposure and set country exposure limits. When the questions asked in our survey are relevant to those posed in these earlier studies, the findings will be compared.

With a promise of confidentiality, three-part questionnaires were dispatched to 122 banks in London. Part A identified the type of respondent bank (merchant, clearing, or foreign bank operating in London). Part B covered CRA-related questions, the analysis of which is dealt with in this section. In Part C, the banks were asked a number of questions about their rescheduled sovereign loans, with the objective of determining the Net Present Value status of these loans. For an analysis of Part C, see Heffernan *et al.* (1985a).

The survey included North American, European, Middle Eastern, Asian and Australasian banking institutions. Of this group, 60 per cent ranked among the world's top hundred by size of deposits and/or capital base in the June 1984 edition of *The Banker*. An overall response rate of 43 per cent was achieved, with eleven banks choosing to remain anonymous. However, a number of banks were excluded from the analysis for one of the following reasons:

(1) The bank did not make sovereign loans.
(2) The bank did not analyse country risk independently.
(3) The questionnaire could not be sent to head office for completion.
(4) The bank was only willing to conduct a personal interview.
(5) The bank refused to answer any questions.

This left a total of 27 banks, on which the analysis of Part B of the questionnaire was based. Foreign banks operating in London made up 85 per cent of the sample, 11 per cent were merchant banks and 4 per cent were clearing banks. Below, the survey responses are analysed under the following headings: responsibility for analysis and related issues; bank approaches to CRA; and the importance of economic and sociopolitical indicators.

RESPONSIBILITY FOR ANALYSIS AND RELATED ISSUES

In the survey, all but two banks reported the employment of specialist credit and/or economic staff to assess country risk. This appears to confirm the finding by Burton and Inoue (1983) that 'in most of the banks in the survey, country risk is evaluated by economists and specialist staff' (p. 42). The approval systems involve either specific credit committees or a hierarchical management process where loans with a relatively high risk or exposure necessitate higher levels of approval authority.

The majority of the banks in this survey had no fixed policy on the frequency with which country risk assessments had to be carried out. As Table 2.6 shows, most country evaluations are reviewed annually, although some banks undertake semi-annual or quarterly reviews. Of the reporting banks, 26 per cent regard their policy as flexible in that the frequency of reviews rises with perceived risk and/or exposure. Again, this finding is similar to the Burton and Inoue study, where a majority of banks undertook regular reviews unless economic or political events prompted an irregular update. From Table 2.6, it will be observed that 30 per cent of the sample responded that they had 'no fixed policy' on frequency of review. This was the typical response when the frequency of review was a function of the given situation, such as the level of risk and/or exposure.

Table 2.6   *Frequency of Country Risk Assessments*

Frequency of review	% of sample
Quarterly	15
Half-yearly	15
Yearly	40
No fixed policy	30

APPROACHES TO COUNTRY RISK ANALYSIS

The banks were requested to indicate which of a number of listed methods described their approach to CRA and, if applicable, to rank them in order of importance. In this survey, all of the respondent banks indicated that they use one or more of the 'systematic' approaches to country risk, that is, they use something other than an ad hoc method in assessing the creditworthiness of a country. This suggests a greater degree of sophistication than that found in two earlier surveys. Goodman (1978) reported that 14 per cent of the participants in the EXIM bank survey had no systematic system, but 62 per cent followed a 'structured qualitative approach'; a standardized format was used to prepare the country report with some statistical analysis included. Another 11 per cent used a 'fully qualitative' approach, preparing country reports based on largely subjective evaluations. Using Goodman's terminology, Mathis and Maslin (1981) found that the majority of their respondents indicated the use of a structured qualitative approach, but one-third relied on qualitative or subjective judgements of a loan officer and 10 per cent reported the use of a 'checklist': a country was awarded a score based on its performance in relation to a number of well-defined variables.

Table 2.7 provides the reader with a detailed percentage breakdown of banks, using the alternative systematic methods listed in our survey.

Table 2.7   *Percentage of Banks Using Alternative Methods of Assessment*

Method	% of banks
1 Statistical model (Discriminant Logit analysis)	22
2 External economic appraisal service	33
3 Standardized country spread sheets	22
4 CRA by in-house economists	93
5 Other	30

In Table 2.7 the percentages do not sum to 100 because 48 per cent of the respondents reported that they use more than one of the above methods; 15 per cent use all of the first four methods listed. It can be seen from Table 2.7 that the vast majority of respondents rely on in-house economists to generate their country reports. Of the banks that chose to rank the different methods in order of importance, the use of in-house economists was consistently ranked as first or second. However, 19 per cent of the respondents commented that assessments provided by account officers (line personnel) were equally important as other designated methods, with only one bank ranking these second to reports made by in-house economists. Table 2.7 shows that 22 per cent of the respondent banks are making use of statistical models or, to employ the Goodman terminology, this group is using 'other quantitative methods'. This is a relatively high percentage when compared with the Goodman paper, where only one of the 37 banks could be placed in this category. In the analysis by Mathis and Maslin, no banks were reported to be following the 'other quantitative' approach. The 'other' category in Table 2.7 is made up of banks reporting the use of assessments made after the return of an account officer to the country in question and/or the employment of business and official (e.g. IMF, BIS) publications in the overall assessment of country risk.

THE IMPORTANCE OF ECONOMIC INDICATORS

In the next part of the questionnaire, the banks were asked to list the five economic indicators perceived by them to be the most important in an assessment of country risk. They were also given an opportunity to rank these indicators. Approximately 15 per cent of the respondents did not identify any economic indicators as being of specific import, with some remarking that the indicators varied with the individual country and therefore no single factor(s) could be singled out. Among the 85 per cent that did identify certain factors, the range was wide and diverse. However, it is possible to group all of the variables listed by the respondents into one of four categories:

(1) Foreign trade indicators.
(2) Variables related to the external debt position.
(3) Domestic economy indicators.
(4) Other.

Some banks listed fewer than five variables, while others listed more than one from each of the above categories. The highest concentration of variables (38 per cent) could be classified in the foreign trade category, followed by the external debt category (29 per cent) and domestic economy indicators (25 per cent). It is worth mentioning that there were some variables cited by respondents that did not fit into the first three groupings listed above. These included the country's ability to respond to shocks, its dependence on the export of primary commodities and/or the import of energy, and the standing of the country within the IMF and/or international capital markets.

Table 2.8 provides a breakdown of the most commonly cited variables and their respective percentages. As may be observed from this table, a few economic variables (e.g. balance of payments and the debt service ratio) were mentioned by a majority of the respondent banks, but there was a considerable variety among the specific variables mentioned, which suggests that there may be a highly subjective component in country risk assessment. In light of the variety of

Table 2.8   *Country Risk Assessment: Economic Indicators Identified by Banks as Important*

Variables most frequently mentioned	% of banks
Current account and balance of payments	87
Debt-service ratio	52
Foreign exchange reserves	39
Economic development/management	39
Inflation/monetary policy	35

responses, it is worth comparing these with the economic variables identified as important in the major statistical studies of sovereign risk analysis by referring back to Table 2.3. Although 52 per cent of the bank respondents cited the DSR as an important economic indicator, only some of the academic studies found it to be statistically significant. However, 87 per cent of the survey respondents identified an external debt indicator as important and 40 per cent listed more than one debt-related variable. In addition, although most of the banks reported the balance of payments as being important, the statistical studies are more specific in their identification of the foreign trade sector variables, with an emphasis on capital flows. Finally, both the survey and the academic studies illustrate a high variance with respect to the economic variables reported as statistically significant in the academic studies.

THE IMPORTANCE OF SOCIOPOLITICAL INDICATORS

The subjective nature of any sociopolitical analysis explains why it is the least well-developed aspect of country risk analysis. However, the analysis of the survey suggests that indicators in this group are important to banks when it comes to their assessment of country risk. Of the respondent banks, 70 per cent ranked sociopolitical factors as being of equal importance to economic factors, 13 per cent identified them as being more important, and 17 per cent responded that they were less important. This finding may be compared with the Burton and Inoue (1983) study, where it was reported that one bank from, respectively, Japan, Europe, and the USA had weighted the relative importance of economic and sociopolitical factors as follows:

	European	Japanese	US
Economic indicators	75%	50%	85%
Sociopolitical indicators	25%	50%	15%

To the extent that the two studies are comparable (our survey includes banks from these geographic regions, but our sample is larger), it appears that, since the Burton and Inoue survey, the banks have shifted to a more equal weighting of the two factors.

When the participants in the survey were asked to name the two most important sociopolitical indicators, the 15 per cent who did not single out any economic factors reacted the same way when it came to this question. The remaining 85 per cent listed the factors shown in Table 2.9 as being important.

Table 2.9 *Country Risk Assessment: Sociopolitical Indicators Identified by Banks as Important*

Indicator	% of banks
1 Political stability – smoothness of transition	74
2 Social unity – educational level	43
3 International relations	22
4 Political system	22
5 Other	9

The responses to this part of the survey are interesting, because they suggest that not only do banks place a considerable weight on these factors when assessing country risk but they also have a clear idea of what sociopolitical indicators contribute to the riskiness of a country. However, countries with sovereign loan problems directly related to social and/or political difficulties are small in number. Most if not all of the recent debt-servicing difficulties can be traced back to economic factors.

The great majority of respondent banks (80 per cent) reported that the method used for sociopolitical assessments was regular visits to the relevant country. It was also ranked as being the most important method in all but one case. As pointed out by Heenan and Rummel (1978), this 'grand tour approach' can create problems because the visitor is subject to the receipt of selective information. On the other hand, the regularity of the visits as reported in our survey (of the banks employing this method, half of them indicated that these trips were made at least semi-annually) may mitigate this problem, because regular visitors would eventually learn the optimal method of gathering information.

The survey revealed that the second most widely used method for sociopolitical assessment was the employment of an external political appraisal service. Of the respondents, 30 per cent reported the use of this method although 75 per cent of this group used these services in conjunction with other methods. The use of acknowledged experts as consultants or advisers was reported by 15 per cent of the participants, though none of the respondents relied on this as their sole source of information.

Having analysed the survey responses in some detail, it is possible to draw the following conclusions:

(1) Compared to earlier surveys, it appears that the international banks have become more systematic in their approach to country risk assessment, with 93 per cent of the sample reporting the use of in-house economists for this purpose and just under one-quarter of the participants relying on sophisticated quantitative techniques to evaluate risk.

(2) The respondent banks vary in their identification of important economic indicators. This is similar to the reported academic work in this field, where the variables identified as being statistic-ally significant vary from study to study.

(3) The banks were in greater agreement when it came to the identification of the sociopolitical indicators important in country risk analysis. The weight the banks attach to these factors is surprising given the predominance of economic factors when one attempts to explain current sovereign loan difficulties.

(4) In the survey, 11 per cent of the respondents admitted that they did not compare their country risk evaluation system with its ex post performance. This is encouraging given that in the Goodman (1978) study only one of the 37 banks reported that it tested the results of its evaluation system. However, the figure is still on the low side.

Conclusions

This chapter began with a review of the approach to sovereign risk analysis taken by two popular financial journals, *Institutional Investor* and *Euromoney*. It was stressed that, although the rankings may provide some indication of sovereign risk, they cannot be interpreted as *measures* of this risk. The statistical approaches of sovereign risk reviewed suffer from a number of statistical problems, but the fundamental difficulty with the approach relates to the lack of theor-etical underpinning for the models. The result of this is that we are left with a variety of economic variables found to be statistically significant (depending on the study) with no clear idea of the true determinants of sovereign risk. The final part of the chapter reviewed how practising international bankers analyse country risk. The survey revealed quite a wide discrepancy between the economic variables identified as important by bankers and those found to be significant in the statistical studies. Bankers also appeared to be concerned about sociopolitical influences, even though there is no hard evidence to suggest that these influence the probability of rescheduling.

Throughout this chapter, the various approaches to sovereign risk analysis have been criticised for their narrow approach to the problem of sovereign risk. This is completely at odds with the general description of the events behind the sovereign debt problems cited in Chapter 1. What is needed is a more general framework of sovereign lending and borrowing, which can be used to identify the key determinants of the demand and supply of sovereign loans. Only then will it be possible to identify the factors contributing to the riskiness of a sovereign loan.

Notes: Chapter 2

1. For example, the Economist Intelligence Unit's International Economic Appraisal Service is employed widely by London-based international banks. It uses one of the most sophisticated statistical models available to identify problem debtor countries.
2. The approach not covered in this chapter is the 'nonparametric approach' employed by Fisk and Rimlinger, 1979, where the prediction of rescheduling is based on historical precedent: a country is predicted to reschedule if the values of certain economic variables are close to the values for a 'cluster' of previous rescheduling cases. Unlike the statistical approaches reviewed in this chapter, there is no attempt to identify statistically significant explanatory variables which influence the probability of rescheduling.

    Dhonte, 1975, employs principal components analysis (PCA) to identify the indicators of 'borrowing conditions' and 'debt involvement'. PCA searches for the degree of dependence that exists between explanatory variables and reduces a large number of correlated variables to a smaller set of statistically independent linear combinations. The Taffler and Abassi study, 1984, uses this method in their development of a discriminant model.
3. See Saini and Bates, 1984.
4. These results are from Feder and Just's 'case c' which excluded the amortization/debt ratio. There were three other cases. Case a included the largest number of explanatory variables and the other three cases were tried with at least one of the explanatory variables in case a omitted; see Feder and Just, 1977, pp. 32–3. Feder, Just and Ross, 1981, also have

more than one model, based on first and second order approximation. The Type I and II errors reported in the text are from Model 1.

5. These likelihood ratio indices are from, respectively, case c and Model 1 of the two studies. See note (4).

6. More detail on Spearman's r (1904) may be obtained from any text on introductory statistics.

3 A Broader Framework for Assessing Sovereign Risk

In Chapter 1, the origins of the current sovereign debt problem were discussed. The importance of the interrelationship between random shocks, the current account deficits of developing countries, and the growth of external debt was identified. The crucial period was the late 1970s and early part of the 1980s, when many developing countries continued to rely on increases in commercial bank lending as their primary source of capital inflow despite greatly increased interest rates, now positive in real terms. These loans were a means of dealing with the continued current account deficit problems and, unlike those of the early 1970s, were less likely to be used for long-term development objectives. This was especially so in the case of the short-term lending, which was rising at a very rapid rate. The growing current account deficits were in turn caused by random shocks to the world economy, which were particularly hard on net debtor countries: debt incurred earlier to finance development was becoming increasingly difficult to repay as current account deficits deteriorated still further. One solution was to borrow more, and this is what many developing countries chose to do. Some evidence suggests domestic adjustment policy in the face of random shocks did improve the ability of some countries to weather the storm. However, the evidence for this is weak, and the overwhelming consideration was the effect of the random shocks to the world economy.

In Chapter 2, the standard approaches to sovereign risk analysis were reviewed. The country rankings produced by the *Institutional Investor* were dismissed as being measures of market attitudes rather than methods of analysis. A good part of Chapter 2 reviewed the statistical models of sovereign risk, because these models are the only systematic approach to sovereign risk analysis currently available. Also, they are being used, either directly or indirectly, by many sovereign lenders. Apart from the serious statistical problems that undermine the credibility of the economic variables found to be statistically significant, Chapter 2 identified a more fundamental problem: these models lacked a theoretical base explaining the origins of sovereign lending and borrowing. The difficulty with this approach is evident when we compare the main conclusions of Chapter 1 with those of Chapter 2. In Chapter 1, we observed the importance of random shocks but, in Chapter 2, the models make no allowance for these. The only exception is the paper by Kharas (1984) but, as has been noted, the final estimating equations do not allow for random shocks. The Kharas model also suffers from a problem common to all the other models, in that it is completely demand side oriented. Yet, in Chapter 1, we observed the importance of the supply side as part of the explanation of the debt problems. Cline (1984) does present a model of demand and supply, but it relates to rescheduling, not to why the loans occurred in the first place. Kletzer (1984) develops a general model of international lending with sovereign risk, but the emphasis is on the problems of asymmetric information related to this kind of borrowing and his specification is quite different from the one presented in this chapter.[1]

This chapter is devoted to developing a general model of the demand and supply of sovereign loans. By so doing, a more general approach to sovereign risk analysis becomes apparent. It is crucial for the sovereign risk analyst to be aware of the critical determinants of supply and demand, because then the factors that can predispose a country to debt-servicing difficulties are fully identified. As this chapter will demonstrate, the explanation of why countries fall into trouble is far more complex than the simple ratio analysis derived from the statistical models of country risk reviewed in Chapter 2. Once the general framework is set up, it is applied to individual country cases, including both problem-free debtor nations and those that have had to reschedule.

The Demand and Supply of Sovereign Loans

In this section a general framework for the demand and supply of sovereign loans is developed. The demand and supply sides are then integrated, and this provides the basis for identifying the factors that could cause a sovereign borrower to encounter debt-servicing problems, to reschedule or to default outright. From Chapter 1, the reader already has some idea of the critical determinants of supply and demand, but these were discussed in terms of the current situation rather than being treated in a more general framework. Technical details are kept to a bare minimum in order to facilitate exposition and because many sovereign risk analysts are not necessarily professional economists. None the less, it is important for this group to realise the importance of taking a broader view of sovereign risk problems than is typically the case. Readers wanting a more technical version of the model are referred to the paper by this author in the *Journal of International Money and Finance* (Heffernan, 1985).

The Supply of Sovereign Loans

The supply of sovereign lending has been largely ignored in the standard approaches to sovereign risk analysis. Like any economic problem, it requires the identification of the determinants of both supply and demand if we are going to be able to explain why some types of sovereign borrowers encounter repayment problems. For example, suppose there is a sudden reduction in the amount of credit available on the international markets when a country is having debt-servicing difficulties because of an adverse current account. The country may well be forced to reschedule. Yet this combination of problems is something largely ignored in the statistical approaches to sovereign risk because of their exclusive focus on the demand side.

Whenever we are developing an economic model it is necessary to specify the assumptions that lie behind the model: we attempt to make these as general as possible in order to ensure a broad application. Of course, it is not possible to cover every possible 'real world' contingency if we are going to be able to derive a general framework. Some readers will think the model has no applicability because the assumptions are simplified versions of what goes on in the 'real world'. This is a common criticism directed at economists, and it is a misunderstanding that needs to be put right. In any economic model, assumptions serve to avoid confusion and provide a starting point for unravelling complex issues. It is much better that they be announced than hidden! In the model presented here, some assumptions are simplistic versions of the 'real world', but they will not greatly undermine our general findings. It is hoped the 'real world' reader will bear with the author throughout the assumptions. Then it will be possible to observe the applicability of the developed framework, despite some of the simplifying assumptions.

We begin with a general assumption, which applies to both the demand and supply sides of international lending. The international economy is divided into a First World group of countries and a Third World group. These terms were first introduced in Chapter 1. The First World consists of a homogeneous group of economies with well-developed capital markets and a supply of capital in excess of domestic requirements. The Third World represents a homogeneous group of less developed countries in which the capital base is insufficient to meet domestic demand. Arbitrage leads to a trade in capital between the two worlds, the First World supplying the Third World until rates of return are equalised. This is a simplifying assumption, since there are several countries that do not fit neatly into either of the two categories. As the reader will come to observe, the general findings will not be affected.

The assumptions specific to the supply side are:

(S1)   For lenders of the First World with excess capital to invest, there are two types of assets from which to choose. There is a safe or risk-free asset and a risky asset, represented by a medium-term or long-term sovereign loan. The difference between the two assets relates to the probability of the lender recovering his or her investment at some future date. The riskless asset is safe because the lender is assured of a certain rate of return on the investment. Good examples of safe assets include certificates of deposits offered by Western banks and many First World short-term government bonds. Of course, these are not 100 per cent safe, but they are close approximations to this. The sovereign loan is risky because the rate of return is uncertain and the lender may not recover his investment. The investor is paid to assume this risk by being offered a higher rate of return on the risky asset. Thus r (the rate of return on the risky asset) is greater than r_* (the rate of return on the safe asset).

This assumption makes the supply of sovereign lending part of an optimal investment decision. The First World lender is risk averse (see S4), has capital to invest, and chooses a portfolio of assets. The risky assets offer a higher rate of return and the investor is attracted to them. But, because the rate of return is uncertain, he can only choose a combination of assets which maximizes his *expected* utility. One of the functions of Western banks is to provide their customers with an asset transformation service through the evaluation of risky assets and portfolio diversification. The individual relies on his friendly banker rather than doing it himself. Some proportion of risky assets in which the bank invests will take the form of lending, including sovereign loans.

The division of assets into one safe and one risky asset and the specification of sovereign lending as a proxy for the risky asset are simplifying assumptions. But our primary objective is to identify the key determinants of the purchase of this type of asset. So it is appropriate to give a simpler version of the portfolio diversification decision. Of course, banks will diversify into a whole range of loans, not just sovereign loans. But, if we were to allow for this, the analysis would become intractable, with an explosion of complexities. The main difference would be that, with many risky assets, the covariance between them would be identified as a determinant of the decision to grant a sovereign loan. More will be said about this once the model is developed.

(S2) No individual action by a First World lender can influence the values of r and $r*$, that is, First World lenders behave as perfect competitors.

(S3) For the risky asset, there are two possible 'states of the world'. The 'good' state obtains when all of the original loan is repaid within the stated time and has an associated probability π. In the 'bad state' the borrower either defaults outright or, by agreement with the lenders, postpones repayment of principal and interest. The probability of this state obtaining is denoted by $(1 - \pi)$. As was noted in Chapter 2, it is quite incorrect to treat outright default and rescheduling as identical events, and this author has no intention of doing so. At a later point in this section, we consider how the different definitions of the two terms affect the determinants of the demand and supply of sovereign lending.

Assumptions S1 and S3 mean that the 'state preference approach'[2] is being used in the derivation of the optimal loan portfolio for First World lenders. It differs from the well-known mean variance or 'modern portfolio' methodology, which assumes that only two variables are influential when an investor chooses among alternative portfolios. These are expected return (the mean of the probability distribution of returns on a portfolio) and risk, proxied by the variance of the probability distribution. Risk is normally classified as either unsystematic (diversifiable) risk or systematic (non diversifiable risk). A portfolio of stocks is defined as 'efficient' when expected returns are maximised subject to a given amount of risk.

As Walter (1981) and Bennett (1984) point out, the application of modern portfolio theory to bank lending requires the acceptance of the idea that banks have portfolios of exposures, the objective of lenders being to maximise the value of these assets subject to a given amount of risk. Sovereign loans may be a part of this efficient loan portfolio. Both authors emphasise the problems associated with any strict application of modern portfolio theory to bank loan portfolios. It is difficult to measure the risks and returns associated with certain types of loans (Walter, 1981, p. 78), a good example being those associated with sovereign loans. Further, unlike stocks, there is an asymmetry in bank lending arising from a limited upside expected return (Bennett, 1984, p. 156). None the less, both authors accept the basic lesson implied by the mean variance approach: for a given amount of risk, diversification of a loan portfolio maximises its expected return.

The application of state preference theory to the derivation of an optimal portfolio is accepted by economists to be the more general of the two methodologies, because it does not restrict investor choice to two determinants: expected return and risk. Rather, this approach begins with the investor choosing among a number of risky assets in order to maximize an underlying expected utility of wealth function. For each risky asset there are a number of states of the world which may or may not obtain. Associated with each state of the world is a *known* pure claim to wealth, redeemed only if the state obtains. The *uncertainty* lies in which state of the world will obtain, although the probability of each state is assumed to be known.

The limitations of the mean variance approach are best seen through consideration of the conditions necessary to make the mean variance and state preference approaches one and the same. It has been shown[3] that one of the following two conditions must be satisfied:

(1)   The underlying expected utility of wealth function must be quadratic if the investor is to be indifferent between any two investments with equal means and equal variances. However, the quadratic utility function implies that the risky asset is an inferior good. In the case of the sovereign loan, this would mean that, as First World wealth increased, investment in risky sovereign loans would decline.

(2)   If the expected utility of wealth function is not constrained to a quadratic form, then it is necessary to assume that the risky asset has a probability distribution of expected returns which is normal. Provided this condition is met, mean and variance are the only two variables which enter the expected utility of wealth function, independent of its form. The problem lies in the assumption that expected returns on a risky loan will follow a normal distribution, especially in the case of a sovereign loan. The asymmetry of returns on lending has been noted by, among others, Bennett (1984).

These limitations suggest that, if the objective is to derive an optimal loan portfolio, the application of state preference theory is the more appropriate of the two methodologies. The underlying expected utility of wealth function is not constrained to any particular form and the variables influencing investor choice need not be confined to the mean and variance of the expected return.

(S4)   The investor is risk averse and, therefore, divides his or her wealth into investment in the safe asset and the risky asset, which in this case is a sovereign loan. The division of the wealth will depend on how risk averse the lender is and on the relative probabilities of the two states obtaining.

(S5)   The lender's estimate of the probability of default is based on the borrower's behaviour with respect to this variable.

These assumptions permit the derivation of a supply of sovereign loans equation, which identifies the explanatory variables that determine the decision to grant a sovereign loan. The actual equation is very complex and, for the purposes of this chapter, unnecessary. Interested readers are referred to Heffernan (1985a). The equation shows that, in all but exceptional cases, the supply of sovereign loans equation has a positive slope, as illustrated in Figure 3.1. The *position* of this curve will be determined by:

(1)   The initial level of First World wealth. A higher level of First World wealth will displace the curve to the right.

(2)   The amount the lender is repaid should the bad state obtain. This can vary from zero in the case of outright default to some positive fraction of the amount that was due to be repaid in the event of rescheduling. The greater is the amount repaid, the higher will be the supply of sovereign loans.

(3)   The degree of risk aversion on the part of the lender. If the lender is highly risk averse, the amount of sovereign lending will be very small. The way the supply side is specified, a higher degree of risk aversion raises the lender's perception of the probability of default. Hence, we can also conclude that a reduction in the probability of default will shift the supply curve to the right.

The *slope* or *gradient* of the curve will be influenced by the degree of risk aversion on the part of the lender, the proportion of the loan

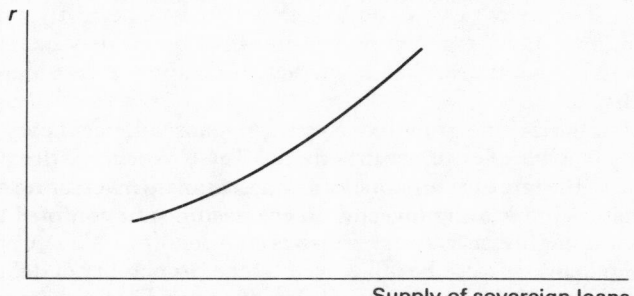

Supply of sovereign loans

Figure 3.1   The supply of sovereign loans.

repaid in the bad state, the rates of return associated with, respectively, the safe asset and the sovereign loan, and the probability of default. Low values for the degree of risk aversion and the probability of default, together with high values for the repayment proportion and the rate of return on the loan will produce a relatively flat sovereign loans supply curve. This means the volume of sovereign loans supplied is more sensitive to changes in r than would be true if the curve had been steeper.

It was noted earlier that in exceptional circumstances the supply curve may not slope upwards from left to right. It is worth exploring this a little further. A high degree of risk aversion can produce a vertical or backward-bending supply curve. This occurs because a high degree of risk aversion makes the investor unresponsive to higher rates of return on the sovereign loan and, normally, this will be found at an upper range of r values. The high degree of lender risk aversion is usually the result of incomplete information on the creditworthiness of the borrower. Poor information will prevent the lender from being able to distinguish between the high risk and low risk sovereign borrower. Offering loans in response to a higher r does not solve the problem because this is more of a deterrent for the low risk than the high risk borrower. The lender may react by ignoring increases in r (a vertical supply curve) or by reducing the amount supplied as r rises (a backward-bending supply curve).

In addition, a very high rate of return on the safe asset ($r*$) could 'crowd out' the supply of sovereign lending because it causes a vertical displacement of the supply curve. The investor gains nothing from supplying sovereign loans because the yield on the safe asset is so high.

These exceptional cases are more likely to cause credit rationing in the supply of sovereign loans, depending on the position of the demand curve for sovereign loans. It is well known that most banks set country limits on the amount they are willing to lend to a given country. The above cases confirm that this is a perfectly rational action in a world of less than perfect information. It may be recalled that none of the approaches discussed in Chapter 2 considers this possibility.

To summarize, the growth of sovereign loans will be an increasing function of the level of wealth in the First World, a decreasing function of the rate of return on the safe asset unless investors exhibit a low degree of risk aversion, and an increasing function of r unless lenders are highly risk averse in sovereign lending. The supply of sovereign loans will also be influenced by the probability of default or rescheduling and the proportion of the loan repaid in the event of the bad state.

The Demand for Sovereign Loans

On the demand side of the model, borrower behaviour must be specified. The following assumptions hold:

(D1)   Each Third World country produces a homogeneous product, Q, with an associated price, P. This is a simplifying assumption, because not all Third World countries produce the same type of goods and most produce several. To make the analysis tractable it is necessary to aggregate in this way, remembering that the objective of the analysis is to identify the key factors that influence the decision to take out a sovereign loan. Nor does it make our findings any less general. The reader may think of Q as being a country's gross national product in volume terms and, if multiplied by P, the GNP (or national income, Y) in terms of value.

A production function describes how factor inputs in the Third World are used to produce the output, Q. The two factors used in the production process are capital and labour. Technical progress is allowed for in the production function and can be either labour-augmenting, increasing the amount of output produced for a given amount of labour, or capital-augmenting, raising the level of production of Q for a given amount of capital.

The production function also has a random disturbance term, denoted by v. This means that the national income of Third World countries may be affected by random shocks. A negative random shock will mean a bad year for the country in terms of national income, while higher national income levels will be the result of a positive random shock.

(D2)   The government of each country wishes to maximize the level of national welfare. The *utility* or *welfare* of the country in any given year depends on the level of national income achieved in that year. At the beginning of each year, the outcome at the end of the year (with respect to national income) is unknown, and this uncertainty means that the borrower is really maximizing an *expected utility function*, i.e. the average utility of each outcome weighted by the perceived probability of that outcome.

(D3)   The borrower is risk averse to low levels of national income. Recall from our description of the national production function that random shocks could affect the level of national income. Had it been neutral to risk, the borrowing country's welfare could have been presented as a linear function of its national income. But, because it is averse to risk, the relationship between its welfare and national income will be curved, as illustrated in Figure 3.2.

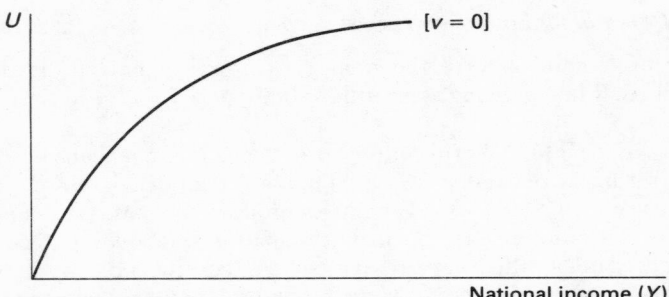

Figure 3.2   Borrower risk aversion to low levels of national income.

In Figure 3.2, the expected utility function of the Third World country appears on the vertical axis and the variable which influences the country's utility is on the horizontal axis. Readers will observe that the curve has a positive gradient. As the level of national income rises, so does the country's level of utility or welfare, but the gradient of the curve grows less steep. This makes the curve concave from below and indicates that this country is risk averse to low levels of national income. Another way of putting this is to say there are diminishing returns to national income: as increasing amounts of income become available, the *rate* of increase in utility begins to diminish. As will be seen below, this risk aversion is one of the critical factors in determining the decision by the borrowing country to default or reschedule. The curve will be shifted by random shocks to national income, upward if positive and downward should there be a negative random shock. It has been drawn for the case of $v = 0$, with no random shock. It should be pointed out that the curve will also shift upward in response to technical progress but, in what follows below, the effects of the random shock receive the most attention, for obvious reasons.

Assumptions D2 and D3 introduce a political dimension to the demand side of the analysis. As all sovereign risk analysts will agree, political factors are often an influential part of the decision to borrow on international capital markets, the economic policies adopted by the government of a borrowing nation, and the decision to reschedule or default outright. However, analysts have failed to make the political dimension an integral part of the sovereign loan framework, a point readily seen if we consider the sovereign risk approaches reviewed in Chapter 2. The specification of a nation's social welfare function on the demand side of the general model eliminates the problems that would arise if political factors were ignored.

(D4)   If the country imports capital, it is assumed to use it to finance the economic development of the country. The capital is forthcoming because, based on expectations of higher future income, investors will anticipate a positive real rate of return on the borrowed capital at some future date. This assumption is a restatement of the development cycle hypothesis described in Chapter 1. If external capital is employed by the developing country, the national income (GNP) will be higher than domestic income or GDP.

(D5)   The demand for external capital by the Third World will be satisfied through sovereign lending. These loans will be raised on the international capital market at interest rate r. Foreign direct investment is ruled out as a means of raising external capital. Readers critical of the simplified nature of this assumption should recall the primary purpose of this chapter, to identify the key determinants of the supply and demand of sovereign loans. If the objective had been to derive optimum foreign gearing ratios for the Third World, then the assumption would have been quite unacceptable, but in the present context it is a convenient simplification. In addition, the forms of financing Third World development in the 1970s (see Chapter 1) lend some empirical support to this assumption.

Assumptions D4 and D5 mean that the Third World will import capital in the form of sovereign loans to finance economic development. However, assumption D3 makes the borrower risk averse to low levels of national income, which in turn can be caused by negative random shocks. Given this risk aversion on the part of the borrower, the country may well attempt to reduce the impact of the random shock by reducing or defaulting on its external repayments. This is where default enters the demand side of the sovereign loan model. Before proceeding any further, it is important to clarify the meaning of default.

(D6)   In what follows below, two types of default are considered. In case A, 'default' is the temporary suspension of debt-service payments, of the sort that has become typical in recent years. The borrower experiences an immediate gain because the reduced charges on external debt will boost national income levels. For the risk averse borrower, the suspension of payments temporarily eases the effects of, say, a negative random shock. The cost to the borrower is in the form of a higher 'penalty' rate of interest paid on the rescheduled debt. In case B, default is defined as outright repudiation. Again, the refusal to repay external debt boosts the borrowing country's level of national income, but the cost of default will be financial autarky, that is, the borrower is denied future access to the international financial markets.

As will be observed below, the determinants of default depend on which case applies. In both cases, the borrower must weigh the costs against the benefits and decide whether the action is appropriate. If the borrower is very risk averse, the country will place a greater weight on the cost of the low income than on the cost of default penalties.

(D7)   The decision to borrow on international capital markets will be taken in terms of two choice variables, the size of the sovereign loan and the probability of default.

Taking these seven assumptions, it is possible to derive a demand for sovereign loans equation. Again, there is no need to produce the technical equation, since the reader is primarily concerned with identifying the variables that influence the demand for sovereign loans. The equation reveals that demand will vary in the following ways:

(1) *Positively*, with national output, its price, capital-augmenting technical progress and, in most cases, labour-augmenting technical change.

(2) *Negatively*, with the domestic supply of capital. As the capital base of the country expands, it will not have to resort to the international capital markets in order to finance its growth. A developing country is more likely to reach this position if the domestic rate of savings is high.

(3) *Negatively*, with the international rental rate on capital. This rate will rise with an increase in the rate of interest on the sovereign loan (r), the price of capital equipment, and the rate of capital depreciation.

Having described the demand and supply side assumptions, it is time to combine the demand and supply equations in order to produce a truly general model of sovereign borrowing and lending decisions.

Integrating the Demand and Supply of Sovereign Loans

The assumptions outlined above permit a full specification of the demand and supply of sovereign loans. In order to complete the derivation of the general framework for sovereign risk analysis, it is necessary to integrate the two sides. This is done by establishing the conditions for market equilibrium and by identifying the variables that will upset this equilibrium.

The term 'market equilibrium' means that demand in a given market is equal to supply. In this case, it refers to the demand for sovereign loans being equal to their supply. A disequilibrium would occur whenever this equality does not hold. Credit rationing is a good example of disequilibrium: the borrower is demanding more credit than the lender is willing to supply. Given the assumptions above, equilibrium in the sovereign loan market will mean that the supply of sovereign loans will equal the Third World's demand for external debt. Although the relevant equations were not reproduced, they can be set equal to each other if market equilibrium prevails. This in turn permits a solution to the system in terms of three *dependent* variables: the rate of change in the supply of sovereign loans (δL), the rate of change in the interest rate (δr) and the rate of change in the probability of default ($-\delta \pi$). The explanatory variables are numerous and best observed by reproducing the system:

$$\delta L = a_1 \delta r* + a_2 \delta A + a_3(\delta B + \delta N) + a_4 \delta \log DK + a_5 \delta \alpha W + a_6 \delta v$$

$$-\delta \pi = b_1 \delta r* + b_2 \delta A + b_3(\delta B + \delta N) + b_4 \delta \log DK + b_5 \delta \alpha W + b_6 \delta v$$

$$\delta r = c_1 \delta r* + c_2 \delta A + c_3 \delta (\delta B + \delta N) + c_4 \delta \log DK + c_5 \delta \alpha W + c_6 \delta v$$

where

a_i, b_i, c_i are the coefficients on the independent variables, $i = 1$, $2, \ldots, 6$. Depending on the coefficient, they are either positive or negative in sign. The components of coefficient are very complex and are not provided in this chapter. The interested reader is referred to Heffernan (1985).

$r*$ is the rate of return on the safe asset

A is capital augmenting technical progress

B is labour augmenting technical progress

N is the factor input, labour

DK is the domestic capital stock

αW is the exogenous part of First World wealth, i.e. that part of wealth not influenced by wealth already invested in sovereign loans

v is the random shock parameter

These three equations represent an integrated sovereign loan system, taking into account all the factors influencing the demand and supply of sovereign loans. In this system, there are seven explanatory or independent variables that will influence equilibrium. These need to be discussed in further detail.[4] In the equations for δL and δr, it will be observed that the equilibrium values of r and L will rise for any of the following changes in explanatory variables:

(1) An increase in the Third World population growth rate (δN), labour-augmenting technical progress, or capital-augmenting technical progress.

(2) A decrease in the level of domestic capital stock.

(3) An increase in the mean value of the random shock parameter.

The equilibrium value of L will fall and r will rise for a change in any of the following variables:

(1) An increase in the safe rate of interest, $r*$.

(2) A decrease in the level of First World Wealth.

(3) An increase in the spread (or variance) of the random shock parameter.

For the sovereign risk analyst, the really interesting equation that comes out of the system is the one for the probability of default ($-\delta \pi$). The system was derived for the case A definition of default, a temporary suspension of payments. Case B will be discussed shortly. This equation corresponds to those derived in the statistical models of Chapter 2. However, it no longer appears as a single equation but as part of a sovereign loan system. An increase in the probability of default will now raise r and lower the supply of sovereign loans. In addition, there are a number of explanatory variables influencing the probability of a temporary suspension of payments. The interesting influences are:

(1) The rate of return on the safe asset. As $r*$ rises, the probability of rescheduling increases.

(2) First World wealth. As αW rises, the probability of rescheduling declines.

(3) The level of domestic capital stock. As DK rises, the probability of rescheduling declines.

(4) The technical progress parameters and the population growth rate. A rise in any of these variables reduces the probability of a temporary suspension of payments.

(5) The random shock parameter, v. A random shock that lowers national income raises the probability of rescheduling. The random shock variable may be interpreted more broadly than it has been up to this point. For example, a random term could be attached to r as well as to Y and the default trigger would be a combination of the two random variables. This modification is particularly important for countries that borrow a large proportion of their external finance at variable rates of interest.

(6) The degree of government risk aversion to low levels of national income. This is not immediately obvious if we look at the system of equations given above. The risk aversion parameter enters the coefficients b_1. At the extreme, when the value for the degree of risk aversion is near its maximum (unity), it will overwhelm all the other variables noted above, because the borrower focuses exclusively on the contingency that, at some future date, a random shock will cause national income to decline to an unacceptably low level. In this extreme case the country borrower is so risk averse that it chooses a lower optimal default level and borrows more now in order to boost income against this future contingency. It should be stressed that, in order for the risk aversion parameter to dominate the system in this way, it will have to be close to its maximum value. Otherwise the other variables will have their usual influence, as discussed in the first five points.

The five variables and the risk aversion parameter are the determinants of the probability of rescheduling. They are quite different from those found to be statistically significant in the models presented in Chapter 2 (see Table 2.3, p. 52). Only the wealth variable is common to the earlier studies, especially those by Taffler and Abassi (1984) and Cline (1984). In the model above, the random shocks to national income and borrower risk aversion could well lead to rescheduling. Similarly, the level of domestic capital stock, the population growth rate and technical progress will influence the decision to reschedule, though these variables will change slowly over time and are unlikely to have the dramatic impact of a random shock or a sudden increase in the degree of risk aversion.

None of the famous 'ratios' typical of the studies presented in Chapter 2 is directly influential. The difference is largely explained by the new approach adopted in this chapter. In the standard statistical approaches, the ratios were 'picked out of a hat' to be tested for significance and it was assumed that a probability of default equation could be estimated in an independent manner. The approach adopted in this section is quite different. The sovereign loan model fully specifies the determinants of the demand and supply of sovereign loans, with the probability of default equation emerging as an endogenous part of the system.

In case B, where default is defined as outright repudiation, the system of equations that emerges is slightly different from the one given for case A. This is because this type of default is much more of a long-run decision for the defaulting country, given that repudiation will result in a protracted period of financial autarky (i.e. exclusion from the world's capital markets) for the nation. Therefore, the decision must be considered in terms of the effect autarky will have on long-term economic growth rates. The derivation of the relevant system of equations is laborious and unnecessary. The main points may be summarized as follows. Outright repudiation will have the immediate impact of boosting mean national income because the country is no longer burdened with external debt repayments. However, subsequent financial autarky may mean that the domestic capital stock is insufficient to equip a growing labour force. The result will be diminishing returns to labour and eventually a lower level of national income per head than would be true if capital could be imported. Eventually, the initial boost to income will be offset by these negative factors. But this will take time and the borrower will have to access how speedy the transition will be. The speed of transition will depend upon the population growth rate, the rapidity with which diminishing returns set in, and the rate of depreciation of the capital stock. The decision to repudiate will also rise with any negative random shock which reduces national income and with the 'discount rate' on future utility. If the latter is high, then outright repudiation is more likely, because the government places a greater weight on the importance of current national income levels.

As a final point, it is worth commenting on the choice of the utility or social welfare function for the borrowing nation. As was noted earlier, it is the social welfare function which permits the analyst to make political factors an integral part of the sovereign loan model. In the specification presented in this section, it was assumed that national income was the independent variable in the utility function of the borrowing nation. An increase in national income raised the country's level of social welfare. However, other independent variables may be assumed to enter the social welfare function, depending on the judgement of the analyst. For example, certain nations may have consumption or consumption per head as their welfare objective. Indeed, this is the assumption made by a number of related studies including Eaton and Gersovitz (1981a, 1981b), Kletzer (1984) and Sachs and Cohen (1982). Compared with the national income specification, the use of these independent variables makes outright repudiation or rescheduling more likely. However, the author believes the national income variable to be more appropriate for most developing countries.

Limitations of the Sovereign Loan Model

Before turning to the applicability of the general framework developed in the previous sections, the limitations of the model should be noted. These relate to the assumptions made earlier in this chapter (see pp. 77–86).

First, no specific allowance was made for the influence of domestic policy on the demand or supply of sovereign loans. In turn, this meant that domestic policy had no influence on the probability of rescheduling or repudiation. Yet, in Chapter 1, there was some weak evidence suggesting domestic policy does make a difference. In the model developed here, the analyst can allow for domestic policy indirectly through the random shock and risk aversion parameters. Domestic policy is going to become increasingly relevant after the country has experienced a random shock which lowers the national income. The country has a number of policy options open to it at this point. A government of a country that is highly risk averse will be more likely to respond to the random shock through expansionary monetary and fiscal policies. If the shock has had a negative impact on the country's current account, these policies will require the country to borrow to finance the current account deficit. The sovereign risk analyst should be looking out for this type of response, which will be characterized by expansionary domestic policies and increased borrowing at a time when the current account deficit is worsening. More will be said about this in Chapter 4. The crucial point is that a *negative random shock* and *risk aversion* are what make domestic policy relevant to the sovereign risk analyst. The only exception to this is the case of a country which has a historical record of irresponsible policy management. The welfare objective of the country will also be important. Countries which place a high priority on consumption per head are more likely to employ expansionary domestic policies to achieve this objective.

Secondly, the only risky asset in the model was sovereign loans. Banks will invest in a number of risky assets. If these had been allowed, the complexity of analysis would have prevented us from focusing on the determinants of sovereign lending. However, in making the decision to grant a sovereign loan, the investor and sovereign risk analyst should consider the relation of this loan to other investments made by the bank if there is a covariance between the loans. For example, a bank making loans to a developing country which relies heavily on a primary commodity should ensure that domestic loans are not concentrated in firms producing the same commodity. If there is a high degree of concentration then a dramatic fall in the price of the commodity will cause both the country and the domestic firms to face liquidity problems simultaneously. Ignoring this potential covariance between different types of loans is a limitation of the model, but it is one which keeps the analysis reasonably simple.

Thirdly, it was assumed that sovereign lending was the only means by which external capital could be imported. As already observed, this assumption would have been most unfortunate had the aim of the model been to identify the determinants of the foreign gearing ratio of a developing country. Although this was not the objective, the implications of allowing for foreign direct investment should be considered. If issues of private equity were used as a means of raising external finance, some of the risk of the investment would be exported to holders of foreign capital. This would reduce the size of the risk borne by the international banking system, which has interdependence between banks as a critical feature. It would also mean domestic residents of the borrowing country would not be bearing 100 per cent of the risk of the public external debt. Equity holdings would also mitigate debt-servicing problems arising from fluctuating exchange rates. External debt-servicing is denominated in a foreign currency, but dividends paid to foreign owners of capital are made in the home currency. Depreciation of the home currency is therefore more painful in the former case. Although these points are worth noting, they do not have a direct impact on the determinants of the supply and demand for sovereign loans identified in the previous sections.

Finally, the sovereign loan model made no provision for moral hazard. This arises when borrowers and lenders are confident of a rescue operation being launched in the event of sovereign loan repayment problems. The effect of moral hazard is to alter the behaviour patterns of lenders and borrowers. The lender would be more inclined to grant riskier loans and the borrower would behave likewise with respect to the use of the funds. This is a problem that deserves serious consideration given the recent rescheduling agreements which have as one of their features IMF intervention. It is considered in some detail in Chapter 5.

Application of the Sovereign Loan Model

In this section the applicability of the framework developed in the previous four sections is reviewed. Unfortunately, a full-scale estimation of the model to test for the significance is not possible because of the complexities involved. To give the reader some idea of the problems, consider the data required for estimation. We would need to collect data on the rate of change in the sovereign loan supply, the risky rate of interest and cases of rescheduling or outright repudiation. Next, we would have to gather data on a sufficient number of random shocks, the proportion of First World wealth held in the safe asset, the Third World's domestic capital stock, the rate of return on the safe asset, rates of technical progress and the labour force growth rate. This is not an impossible task, but it would not be appropriate for this book. The sovereign risk analyst is concerned with the applicability of the model to the 'real world' and it is possible to review this issue without resorting to a full-scale econometric model. In what follows below, this is accomplished in two ways. The model's ability to explain the current problems is reviewed and then some individual country cases are explored.

Application of the Sovereign Loan Model to Current Financial Problems

Some readers may have already discerned the key value of the general framework presented in the previous sections, namely its allowance for random shocks and borrower risk aversion as factors influencing the probability of temporary suspension of debt repayments or outright default. It may be recalled from Chapter 1 that much of the recent financial problems relating to rescheduling of sovereign debt can be traced to three random shocks: the dramatic rise in world interest rates, the world recession and the change in the relative price of oil, the effect of the latter depending on whether the country was a net oil importer or exporter. Clearly it is exactly these types of shocks that eventually influence the borrower's decision to reschedule or repudiate in the sovereign loan model.

However, this is not the only advantage of the general approach. To see this, return to the determinants of the demand and supply of sovereign lending. On the demand side, there were a number of important variables, including aggregate price, output, the international capital rental rate (which will rise with r, the rate of interest on the sovereign loan), the domestic capital base and the degree of borrower risk aversion to low levels of national income. If the borrowing country is to demand the optimal amount of sovereign debt, it must accurately forecast the future values for these variables. This is a daunting task. Let us consider the implications of the failure to forecast accurately one of the variables, the real rate of interest.

At the time when many of the sovereign loan agreements were reached, the future increase in the interest rate was not anticipated. It was not until after 1976 that real rates of interest turned positive, rising rapidly after 1978. This has created serious front-loading problems for many of the debtor nations: 'up front' annual repayments rose dramatically after sharp increases in the nominal rate of interest. If the increase in these rates of interest had been the result of a rise in inflationary expectations which were later fulfilled, then the optimal level of sovereign borrowing would not be affected because the front-loading would be offset by an annual decline in the real burden of debt.

Unfortunately, the higher world rates of interest could not be explained solely by higher expectations of inflation. Other factors, such as increased risk premiums and, more important, a tight monetary policy in most of the First World (which put pressure on $r*$, the safe rate of return) also contributed to a rise in r. To the extent that the rise in r in the late 1970s is explained by these factors, it should have signalled a need for the Third World to cut back on, rather than raise, their external debt commitments. It may well be that borrowers and lenders alike confused the reasons for the rise in world interest rates, even though these had quite different implications for the optimal level of external debt.

The remarks in the previous two paragraphs apply to the proportion of borrowing country sovereign loans subject to variable rates of interest. As will be observed in the next section, this figure varies considerably from country to country. Hence, for some borrowers, the impact of the interest rate shock was very small. On the other hand, sovereign borrowers which managed to negotiate fixed interest loans were exposed to a risk that real interest rates might fall well below the negotiated fixed rate.

For the Third World borrowing countries producing primary products other than oil, the dramatic fall in the prices of these primary products from the mid-1970s onwards created yet another problem on the demand side. The success of OPEC raised the expectation on the part of many primary commodity producers that similar cartels could be formed among the producers of other primary products. This, in turn, raised expectations of future export earnings, which seemed to justify higher levels of external borrowing. Unfortunately, this proved not to be the case. The serious world recessions in 1974–6 and 1979 were the main factor undermining the effectiveness of the cartels. Commodity prices plummeted. Between the third quarter of 1974 and the fourth quarter of 1975, non oil primary commodity prices fell in real terms by 30 per cent and, between the first quarter of 1981 and the fourth quarter of 1982, by 21 per cent. These declines were not accompanied by proportionate fall in the international rental rate on capital. The demand side of the sovereign loan model suggests these events should have acted as a signal to cut back on external borrowing. Instead, we have observed a steady rise.

Turning to the supply side, several factors give cause for concern. First, a world recession which lowers First World wealth will reduce the volume of sovereign lending. Secondly, if the spate of reschedulings make the lender more risk averse, fewer sovereign loans will be supplied even if r rises. There is some evidence to suggest that this has been the case since the end of 1982.[5] Finally, the model assumed that the proportion of the sovereign loan repaid in the bad state was a known parameter. However, banks may revise their estimates of this parameter because of all the rescheduling. If banks perceive that they have come out badly they will revise down their estimates of repayment and this in turn could have an adverse effect on sovereign loan supplies. A study by this author and others (Heffernan *et al.*, 1985a) suggests that, in terms of net present value, some banks have done rather well while others have experienced net present value losses.

As was stressed in Chapter 2, the rescheduling packages represent new loan agreements between borrower and lender. Some readers may be wondering whether this represents an inconsistency with the predictions of the model. The answer is no if we accept the interventionist role played by the IMF. Third-party intervention was not allowed for in the sovereign loan model. To use Cline's terminology (1984, p. 72), 50 per cent of net new lending to developing countries in 1983 was *involuntary* in the sense that only banks already exposed in the country agreed to increase their exposure. The IMF insisted on increased exposure by the banks if it was to help in the rescheduling packages. In the absence of this intervention, it is questionable whether the increased supply of sovereign loans would have taken place to the extent that it did. The role of the IMF is explored in greater detail in Chapter 5.

Application of the Sovereign Loan Model to Individual Country Cases

In this part of Chapter 3, the demand side of the general framework developed earlier (see pp. 83–6) is applied to individual country cases. The countries chosen for review come from the IMF's list of 25 major debtor countries (see Chapter 1), although not all of them have rescheduled. Attention is confined to those countries that have rescheduled as opposed to repudiating their external debt outright, since the latter is a rare event. The countries chosen are classified as follows:

GROUP I:

Developing countries that have rescheduled in the period 1975 to 1980 or in the years 1981, 1982 and 1983 and are net oil exporters:

Mexico
Nigeria

Mexico is not included in the IMF's classification of 'oil exporting' developing countries but is in the subgroup 'net oil exporters' in the non oil developing country category.

GROUP II:

Developing countries that have rescheduled between 1975 and 1980 or in 1981, 1982 or 1983 and are net oil importers:

Brazil
Turkey
Zaire

Each of these countries falls into a separate IMF subgroup within the non oil classification. Brazil is a major exporter of manufactures, Turkey is a middle income country which exports primary commodities and Zaire is a 'low income' country with a per capita GDP that did not exceed $350 in 1978.

GROUP III:

Developing countries that have not rescheduled:

Egypt: like Mexico, a net oil exporter in the non oil developing country group.

India: classified in the low income subgroup of non oil developing countries.

Israel: classified as a major exporter of manufactures in the non oil developing country group.

Republic of Korea: classified in the same group as Israel.

Thailand: appears in the primary product export subgroup of the non oil developing countries.

In the author's opinion, this sample of developing countries is fairly representative of countries that have or have not rescheduled. The economic profile of each country will be presented with the object of identifying the key features of the country which have influenced its ability to meet its debt-servicing obligations. In keeping with the sovereign loan model, attention is focused on the effects of the three random shocks (real interest rates, world recession and oil prices) and how these have affected the ability of the countries to service their external debt. Domestic policies of the individual countries are also reviewed. The impact of each of the shocks and domestic policy will be measured by examining data on the following:

(1) *Increased Rates of Interest:*
The impact of this is studied by looking at the percentage of external loans subject to variable rates of interest.

(2) *World Recession:*
The effects of the downturn in the world economy are captured by studying the country's terms of trade (the ratio of export prices to import prices) and the composition of exports and imports.

(3) *Oil Prices:*
The impact of the fluctuation in oil prices in the 1970s is captured by several indicators, depending on whether or not the country is a net oil exporter or importer of oil. If a non oil developing country, the effect of oil on the country's import bill is relevant. For a net exporter, it is the percentage contribution of oil exports to total exports and the impact of oil price rises on expectations of future economic development and borrowing patterns that are important.

(4) *Domestic Policy:*
The domestic policy of the country is proxied by three variables, the rate of inflation, the fiscal deficit as a percentage of GNP, and real GDP growth rates.

Group I

MEXICO

Mexico is still classified by the IMF as a net oil exporter in the non oil developing country group because it does not quite meet the strict criteria (see Chapter 1) laid down by the IMF for classification as an oil exporting developing country. However, oil now dominates Mexico's exports, making the country dependent on sustained oil price rises for oil revenues. The change in Mexico's composition of exports since the mid-1970s is evident from Table 3.1, which is based on reviews by the Economist Intelligence Unit (EIU).

Table 3.1 illustrates the dramatic change in Mexico's composition of exports. Mexico has emerged from being a reasonably well diversified exporter of primary goods and agricultural products to a country that relies heavily on one primary product for export revenues.

Table 3.1   *Composition of Main Exports (Percentage of Main Export Value), 1975 and 1983, Mexico*

1975		1983	
Crude oil	39.0	Crude oil	84.0
Coffee	16.5	Automotive	4.1
Sugar	12.0	Food/beverages/tobacco	3.6
Cotton	11.3	Petrol products	3.5
Shrimps	8.0	Chemicals	2.6
Tomatoes	6.7	Metallic minerals	1.15
Fluorspar	4.4	Machinery and equipment	1.06
Fresh/frozen meat	0.95		

Source: EIU, *Quarterly Economic Review of Mexico* Annual Supplements 1977 and 1984.

Thus, Mexico's track-record on the current account will depend on world oil prices. This can be illustrated by examining Mexico's current account performance through the 1970s and early 1980s (see Table 3.2).

For Mexico, the sharp increase in oil prices at the end of 1973 and again at the end of 1978 signalled that, provided these prices were sustained, expectations of growth for the Mexican economy were good. It was rational for borrower and lender alike to increase

Table 3.2   *External Indicators, Mexico*

	1973–8 (annual average)	1979	1980	1981	1982	1983
Peso/SDR[1]	19.63	29.46	29.87	28.91	62.3	128.4
Current account ($bn)	− 2.8	− 5.5	− 8.1	− 13.9	− 2.9	
Capital account[2] ($bn)	3.8	5.1	12.9	23.2	6.3	
Terms of trade	Not available for Mexico					

Note 1: The peso/SDR exchange rate gives the period average peso currency value of the SDR. Since July 1984, the SDR has been determined daily by the IMF on the basis of a basket of currencies, with each currency assigned a weight. An increase in the peso/SDR rate implies a depreciation in the value of the peso. The national currency/SDR (period average) rate will be quoted for all countries unless otherwise stated.

Note 2: The capital account figures exclude reserves. This will be the case for all countries unless otherwise stated.

Source: IMF *International Financial Statistics Yearbook*, 1984. Unless otherwise stated, country tables on external indicators come from this source.

commercial lending to this country. However, Mexico's changed composition of trade made the country's balance of payments vulnerable to any decline in oil prices, and this began after 1981. With large current account deficits in 1980 and 1981, the capital account surplus almost doubled between 1980 and 1981 even though by this time oil prices were expected to decline. This kept the exchange rate at artificially high levels until February 1982, when the government devalued the peso against the dollar.

Given Mexico's export profile, the primary effect of the world recession in 1981–2 was through the impact on oil prices. External borrowing from private creditors continued to rise, as Table 3.3 reveals.

Table 3.3   *External Debt, Mexico*

	1973	1975	1977	1978	1979	1980	1981	1982
DOD ($bn)	5.6	11.5	20.8	25.6	29.2	33.6	42.7	50.4
of which:								
(%)								
Official creditors	29	20	15	13	13	13	12.5	14
Private creditors	71	80	85	87	87	87	87.5	86
VIL (%)	40	51	53	59	69	71	75	76
Con.L (%)	5.7	3.4	2.0	1.6	1.5	1.2	1.0	0.9

Abbreviations:
DOD: disbursed public or publicly guaranteed debt outstanding. Figures are in billions of US dollars and have been rounded off. Unless otherwise stated, this will be done for all other countries.
VIL: the proportion of disbursed debt subject to variable rates of interest.
Con.L: the concessional loan proportion of disbursed debt.
Source: World Bank, *World Debt Tables* 1983–4. Unless otherwise stated, country tables on external debt come from this source.

In nominal terms, Mexico's sovereign debt increased at an average annual rate of 25 per cent over the period. This relatively high growth rate and the terms of the increased commercial lending made Mexico vulnerable to the second random shock, the rise in real rates of interest. For an increasing proportion of the disbursed debt was subject to variable rates of interest and a falling proportion represented concessional loans. Further, when Mexico began to experience current account problems in 1981, the proportion of lending from official sources actually declined.

On the domestic policy front, Mexico was committed to high rates of economic growth throughout the 1970s and into the 1980s. This was reflected in the high rate of economic growth, and the rise in the fiscal deficit as a percentage of GDP. The rapid rise in the inflation rate from the late 1970s onwards reflected the impact of expansionary policies on aggregate demand. This also increased the demand for imports prior to and after the oil price began to decline. The relevant figures are summarized in Table 3.4.

Many residents of Mexico appeared to see the writing on the wall before the international banking community. In 1981 there was a capital outflow of $8.4 billion in response to the overvalued currency. This figure rose to nearly $9 billion in early 1982, even though the peso was devalued in February 1982 and a number of domestic measures to curb inflation undertaken.

To summarize, Mexico's reliance on oil as the main source of export revenues and the high proportion of disbursed debt subject to variable rates of interest made it highly vulnerable to the shocks to the world economy. While the price of oil was high, Mexico's borrowing pattern was justified, but continued increases in borrowing after the price began to decline were inconsistent with the objective of borrowing to

Table 3.4   *Domestic Policy Indicators, Mexico*

	1973–8 (annual average)[1]	1978–9	1979–80	1980–1	1981–2	1982–3
Real GDP growth (%) (1980 prices)	5.5	9.2	8.3	8.0	− 0.55	− 4.96

	1974–8 (annual average)	1979	1980	1981	1982	1983
Fiscal deficit as a % of GNP	3.7	3.4	3.2	7.0		
Price index[2] (1980 prices)	44.4	79.0	100	128	203	410

Note 1: As the different countries are reviewed, readers will note the variation in the years included in the computation of the annual averages. This is explained by limitations in the availability of data from country to country, and could not be avoided.

Note 2: This is the consumer price index cited in the IMF *International Financial Statistics*. It is used for all countries cited.

Sources: Figures on the deficit are from the IMF *Government Financial Statistics Yearbook*, 1984. All other figures are from the IMF *International Financial Statistics Yearbook*, 1984. The same sources are used for all the countries reviewed.

Table 3.5 *Composition of Main Exports (Percentage of Main Export Value), 1975 and 1981, Nigeria*

1975		1981	
Crude petroleum	95.0	Petroleum	99.2
Cocoa	3.7	Cocoa	0.8
Palm kernels	0.38		
Tin	0.35		
Rubber	0.31		
Timber	0.09		
Groundnut products	0.02		

Source: EIU, *Quarterly Economic Review of Nigeria* Annual Supplements 1977 and 1984.

finance development based on expectations of higher future income streams. Domestic economic policies, reflecting Mexico's concern over increasing the growth rate of national income exacerbated the problems arising from external difficulties. In August 1982, Mexico suspended payment of principal on foreign debt for 90 days. This was followed by an agreement to reschedule in 1983.

NIGERIA

Nigeria is classified by the IMF as a developing country oil exporter: oil exports consist of a minimum of 100 million barrels a year and account for at least two-thirds of total exports. Table 3.5 summarizes Nigeria's composition of exports for 1975 and for 1981 (the latest year available).

Unlike Mexico, Nigeria has always relied heavily upon one primary commodity export, making the country vulnerable to the effects of world economic recession, which impact on the prices of primary

Table 3.6 *External Indicators, Nigeria*

	1973–8 (annual average)	1979	1980	1981	1982	1983
Naira/SDR	0.75	0.78	0.71	0.72	0.74	0.77
Current account ($bn)	0.76	1.67	4.25	− 5.8	− 7.3	
Capital account ($bn)	3.4	1.23	− 0.55	1.2	5.5	
Terms of trade (1975 = 100)	94.1	122.6	185.2	209.7		

Table 3.7   *External Debt, Nigeria*

	1973	1975	1977	1978	1979	1980	1981	1982
DOD ($bn)	1.2	1.1	0.9	2.3	3.2	4.1	4.9	6.1
of which: (%)								
Official creditors	54	68	94	39	29	24	20	19
Private creditors	46	32	6	61	71	76	80	82
VIL (%)	0.8	0.7	0.6	60	69	75	77	74
Con.L (%)	24.7	32.8	44.1	18.2	13.2	10.5	7.6	5.5

products. There was no dramatic change in Nigeria's composition of exports during the 1970s, except for the greater concentration on oil production at the expense of other products. Table 3.6 illustrates the impact of this dependence on Nigeria's external indicators.

The naira fell only slightly against the SDR from 1981, even though Nigeria was recording a serious balance of payments deficit from 1981. The IMF has attempted to persuade Nigeria of the necessity of further devaluation, but so far IMF advice has been ignored. Lack of data prevents the illustration of the deterioration in the current account since 1982. Unlike Mexico, no large-scale devaluation has taken place. Capital inflows continued through the early 1980s, as confirmed in Table 3.7, where public and publicly guaranteed disbursed debt outstanding rose by almost $2 billion between 1980 and 1982.

Table 3.8   *Domestic Policy Indicators, Nigeria*

	1973–8 (annual average)	1978–9	1979–80	1980–1	1981–2
Real GDP growth (%) (1980 prices)	4	6	0.4	− 5	− 2.2

	1973–4	1975	1976	1977	1978
Deficit as a % of GNP	surplus	NA	6.2	9	5.2

	1973–8	1979	1980	1981	1982	1983
Price index (1980 = 100)	52.7	89.8	100	120.9	130	156

Table 3.9   *Composition of Main Exports (Percentage of Main Export Value), 1974 and 1983, Brazil*

1974		1983	
Raw sugar	17.5	Soya	11.7
Soya beans	16	Coffee	10.6
Coffee beans	15	Transport goods	8.7
Iron ore	10	Iron ore, manganese	7.1
Machinery	7.8	Machinery	4.9
Crystal and refined sugar	5.5	Footwear	3.7
Vegetable oils	4.7	Cocoa	2.5
Processed foods	4.6		
Cocoa	3.8		
Maize	2.4		
Shoes	2.1		
Tobacco	1.8		
Cotton	1.7		
Steel products	1.3		
Meat	1.2		
Manganese	0.89		

Source: EIU, *Quarterly Economic Review of Brazil* Annual Supplements 1976 and 1984.

Also notable is the dramatic increase in the percentage of DOD owed to private creditors after 1978. This reflected expectations of relatively high oil prices and Nigeria's favoured borrowing position as a member of OPEC. Like Mexico, commercial borrowing by Nigeria continued to increase at a rapid rate, even after oil prices began to decline. In 1978, the sudden jump of disbursed debt subject to variable rates of interest increased Nigeria's vulnerability to the real interest rate shock.

Table 3.10   *External Indicators, Brazil*

	1975–8 (annual average)	1979	1980	1981	1982	1983
Cruzeiros/SDR	13.0	34.81	68.6	109.8	198.2	616.9
Current account ($bn)	− 5.9	− 10.48	− 12.81	− 11.8	− 16.3	
Capital account ($bn)	7.3	6.5	9.4	12.7	7.5	
Terms of trade (1980 = 100)	133.6	120.5	100.0	85.0	82.0	81.0

The domestic policy profile (see Table 3.8) is similar to that of Mexico. Despite negative growth rates from the beginning of the 1980s, inflation rates are rising. Unfortunately, the data on the fiscal deficit is too dated to permit an opinion to be formed.

Nigeria reached a rescheduling agreement with commercial creditors in 1983. The profile was very similar to that of Mexico and fits well into the sovereign loan model.

Group II

BRAZIL

Brazil is classified by the IMF as a net oil importer in the subgroup of major exporters of manufactures. The composition of exports has not changed very much between 1975 and 1982, as Table 3.9 illustrates.

The IMF classifies Brazil as a non oil exporter of manufactured goods. In 1974, it will be observed that primary commodities made up approximately 60 per cent of Brazil's main exports. The figures for 1983 are not strictly comparable with those for 1974 because they represent the exports as a percentage of total exports, not just main exports. None the less, in 1983, three primary commodities accounted for more than a quarter of Brazil's exports, although manufactured goods exports have clearly increased in significance. Brazil's export composition has become more diversified and this should lessen the impact of world economic shocks.

Something not revealed in the figures cited for exports is the key contributor to Brazil's import bill: fuels. In 1983, 53 per cent of Brazil's total value of imports consisted of fuels and lubricants. Roughly the same figure can be quoted for the period 1978 to 1980. The 1974 oil price shock increased the current account deficit in Brazil to 90 per cent of export earnings. However, the government continued with a high growth strategy, meaning there was little adjustment in

Table 3.11   *External Debt, Brazil*

	1973	1975	1977	1978	1979	1980	1981	1982
DOD ($bn) of which: (%)	7.5	13.8	21.9	30.0	35.5	39.5	44.5	47.6
Official creditors	36	29	23	19.5	18	17	17	17
Private creditors	64	71	77	80.5	82	83	83	83
VIL (%)	34	51	54	56	59	61	67	70
Con.L (%)	21	13	8	6	5	4	3.5	3.2

the Brazilian economy to the change in the relative price of oil. This created rising current account deficits throughout the 1970s and large capital inflows to finance the growth policy. Table 3.10 illustrates the movements of the external indicators and Table 3.11 shows the rapid rise in external debt through the period.

The terms of trade deteriorated substantially after 1980, even though oil prices began to decline in 1981–2. Brazil's exports suffered from the world recession, which lagged behind the second oil price increase in late 1978. Even so, Brazil's export performance in 1980 improved enough to reduce the size of the current account deficit in 1981. Note that, despite the falling TOT, capital inflows continue to rise, as did the burden of external debt.

The average annual growth rate in Brazil's nominal DOD was 20 per cent. As in the case of Nigeria and Mexico, the data on external debt reveal a falling proportion of disbursed debt in the form of concessional loans and a rising proportion subject to variable rates of interest, making Brazil vulnerable to the interest rate shock.

With the exception of uncontrollable inflation, Brazil's economy has performed reasonably well (see Table 3.12). Growth rates were healthy until the beginning of the 1980s. As we have seen, however, Brazil's commitment to high growth rates was at the expense of an increasing external debt and adjustment of the economy to higher oil prices. This made Brazil highly vulnerable to two external shocks at the end of the decade and, in addition, exports suffered following world recession.

Table 3.12   *Domestic Policy Indicators, Brazil*

	1973–8 (annual average)	1978–9	1979–80	1980–1	1981–2	1982–3
Real GDP growth (%) (1980 prices)	7.1	6.4	7.2	– 1.56	0.93	– 3.2

	1973–8 (annual average)	1979	1980	1981	1982	1983
Price index (1980 = 100)	18.3	54.7	100	205.6	407	985
Deficit as a % of GNP	8.3	0.57	2.4	2.4	2.7	

Table 3.13   *Composition of Main Exports (Percentage of Main Export Value), 1976 and 1983, Turkey*

1976		1983	
Cereals and leguminous seeds	37	Fruit, vegetables and nuts	30
Cotton	22	Cereals	19.3
Fruit, vegetables and nuts	19	Livestock and animal produce	19.2
Tobacco	12	Tobacco	12
Minerals	5.4	Cotton	9.8
Livestock and animal produce	3.7	Minerals	9.5

Source: EIU, *Quarterly Economic Review of Turkey* Annual Supplements 1978 and 1984.

TURKEY

Unlike Brazil, Turkey is classified as a primary commodity exporter in the non oil developing country group. Table 3.13 summarizes Turkey's main sources of export revenue.

This table demonstrates Turkey's dependence on the export of agricultural products for export revenue. A good part of Turkey's main exports are necessities and are unlikely to be much affected by the effects of world recession.

Like Brazil, Turkey's import bill is dominated by petroleum imports. In 1976, petroleum and petroleum products made up 27 per cent of the main composition of imports. In 1983, this figure was 46 per cent. In a recent article ('Turkey: a new financial dawn', Supplement to *Euromoney*, September 1984) a deputy to the governor of the Bank of Turkey candidly admits that the country's economic position was undermined by the slow adjustment (over seven years) to the change in the relative oil price. This increased Turkey's vulnerability, just as it had for Brazil. However, Turkey has rescheduled its external

Table 3.14   *External Indicators, Turkey*

	1973–8 (annual average)	1979	1980	1981	1982	1983
Liras/SDR	20.2	40.2	99	131	179.5	241
Current account ($bn)	− 1.3	− 1.4	− 3.2	− 1.9	− 0.79	
Capital account ($bn)	1.6	0.65	2.1	1.25	1.22	
Terms of trade (1980 = 100)	141.9	125	100	94	88	86

debt on five separate occasions (in 1959, 1965, 1978, 1979 and 1980). The rescheduling in the 1950s was between Turkey and a number of western nations. Balance of payments problems led to an extension of debt relief by the consortium of Turkey's official creditors. It is interesting to investigate the reasons why Turkey rescheduled relatively early among the debtor countries. To explore the possible reasons, Turkey's external indicators, proxies for domestic policy and external debt data are summarized in Tables 3.14 to 3.16.

These figures illustrate steadily declining terms of trade from 1980 and a substantially depreciating currency through the entire period, even though in certain years the capital inflow more than made up for the current account deficit. It appears that the currency was allowed to depreciate in line with the balance of payments.

Turning to the external debt data for Turkey, Table 3.15 illustrates a steady rise in external disbursed debt through the period, at an average annual rate of 18 per cent.

As Table 3.15 illustrates, the Turkish case is somewhat different from that for previous countries reviewed here. There was a much less rapid growth rate in private credit, as a proportion of external debt and the percentage of external debt subject to variable rates of interest is comparatively small.[6] In addition, the greatest proportion of the debt was rescheduled in the period 1975 to 1980 (before the second world recession and the steep rise in real interest rates) when some $6.6 billion was rescheduled, $4.7 billion of this being the rescheduling of an aid consortia agreement.

Nor do Turkey's domestic policy indicators shed much light on why Turkey rescheduled at an early date (see Table 3.16). Other than a high rate of inflation, there is nothing in the domestic policy proxies to suggest a need to reschedule, particularly in the mid-1970s.

Therefore, from what we can observe, the Turkish case does not appear to be explained by the sovereign loan model developed in this

Table 3.15 *External Debt, Turkey*

	1973	1975	1977	1978	1979	1980	1981	1982
DOD ($bn)	2.9	3.2	4.3	6.4	11.0	13.5	13.97	15
of which: (%)								
Official creditors	94	95	85	86	66	62	65	65
Private creditors	6	5	15	14	34	38	35	35
VIL (%)	0.5	0.8	7.8	6.7	29.4	25.5	25	NA
Con.L (%)	85	79	65	48	33	32	32	31.6

Table 3.16   *Domestic Policy Indicators, Turkey*

	1973–8 (annual average)	1978–9	1979–80	1980–1	1981–2	1982–3
Real GDP growth (%) (1980 prices)	5.35	2.6	− 1.07	4.0	4.5	3.4

	1973–6 (annual average)	1977	1978	1979	1980	1981
Deficit as a % of GNP	0.56	6	2.5	6.2	3.6	1.8

	1973–8 (annual average)	1979	1980	1981	1982	1983
Price index (1980 = 100)	17	47.6	100	136.6	178.7	230.7

chapter. There is an explanation for this apparent failure. The data on debt exclude short-term foreign loans. This type of lending is what prompted the 1977 crisis and an approach to the IMF in early 1978. A scheme which created Convertible Turkish Lire Deposits permitted foreign residents to convert hard foreign currency into lira and deposit the lira in a commercial bank in Turkey. Nominal interest rates were comparatively high and the central bank guaranteed the deposits against any exchange rate loss. By the end of 1977, these deposits accounted for more than one-third of short-term debt, which in turn represented 52 per cent of total external debt. All this is missed when one relies on the World Bank's *World Debt Tables*. This debt was being used to finance a relatively high real GDP growth rate and the subsidy which kept the domestic price of oil well below world prices.

Therefore, the events of the mid-1970s do fit the sovereign loan model. What we have is a government committed to relatively high real rates of economic growth at a time when the oil price shock would normally have prevented this from being achieved.

ZAIRE

Zaire is another country that rescheduled its external debt comparatively early, in the second half of the 1970s. Official creditors

Table 3.17 *Composition of Main Exports (Percentage of Main Export Value), 1975 and 1982, Zaire*

1975		1982	
Cotton	46.0	Copper	50.3
Copper	30.3	Gold	17.4
Cobalt	6.4	Cobalt	11.5
Coffee	4.3	Coffee	7.4
Diamonds	3.5	Diamonds	5.2
Palm oil products	2.6	Zinc	2.7
Zinc	2.0	Silver	1.7
Cassiterite	1.3	Manganese	1.2
Oil Cake	0.98	Cassiterite	1.1
Gold	0.88	Rubber	0.52
Silver	0.43	Palm oil products	0.45
Tea	0.36	Cocoa	0.29
Rubber	0.25	Tea	0.14
Cocoa	0.24		
Manganese	0.14		
Timber	0.7		

Source: EIU, *Quarterly Economic Review of Zaire* Annual Supplements 1978 and 1984.

agreed to a total of four reschedulings in early 1976, twice in 1977, and again in 1979. Two more reschedulings have taken place in the 1980s, the most recent being in 1983.

Zaire is classified in the 'low income' subgroup of the non oil developing countries, and it is a country earning a subsistence level of GNP. This tends to increase the sensitivity of the government to shocks which threaten what is already a low level of national income. A review of Zaire's principal exports underlines its vulnerability to sudden changes in the price of primary commodities.

As we can see from Table 3.17, Zaire relies on exports of primary products for export revenues. Since 1975, Zaire has grown less diversified in these exports. In 1982, mineral products made up 94 per cent of main exports, compared with 45 per cent in 1975. The export of animal and vegetable products (especially cotton) has become an insignificant part of Zaire's exports. The reduced diversification has made Zaire subject to fluctuations in world mineral prices, especially copper and gold. These in turn tend to follow a world recession.

Table 3.18 summarizes Zaire's external indicators. The lack of recent data prevents us from forming a clear picture of what has happened since 1980. Worthy of note is the sharp decline in capital

Table 3.18   *External Indicators, Zaire*

	1973–8 (annual average)	1979	1980	1981	1982	1983
Zaires/SDR	0.8	2.4	3.7	5.2	6.4	13.8
Current account ($mn)	− 558.5	322.4	332.4			
Capital account ($mn)	699.0	103.0	69.0			
Terms of trade	NA					

inflows, which began in 1978. The current account is in deficit for much of the time, moving with the world recession, an unsurprising trend given Zaire's dependence on mineral export revenues.

Information on Zaire's import composition is not available after 1976. At that time, energy made up 15.6 per cent of Zaire's main imports, processed materials (36 per cent) and consumer goods (28 per cent) being other major contributors. At this time, Zaire's vulnerability to the oil price shocks would affect the country's ability to repay sovereign loans.

Table 3.19 gives the external debt data for Zaire. Though the average annual rate of increase in external debt was 16 per cent, Zaire was the only country among the rescheduling nations reviewed to have experienced an increase in the proportion of lending from official sources. Nor has there been the dramatic increase in the proportion of loans subject to variable rates of interest typical of the other countries.

Table 3.19 reveals that, if anything, the terms on which external debt has been negotiated improved over the last decade, making Zaire far less subject to the interest rate shock than any other country. The amount of external disbursed debt outstanding has declined since 1980. The figures indicate that private lenders have been cautious in

Table 3.19   *External Debt, Zaire*

	1973	1975	1977	1978	1979	1980	1981	1982
DOD ($bn) of which: (%)	0.9	1.72	2.84	3.5	4.0	4.2	4.1	4.0
Official creditors	19	28	37	41	46	62	63	68
Private creditors	81	72	63	59	54	38	37	32
VIL (%)	39	27	20	15.5	14	12	11.6	12
Con.L (%)	15	19	23	24	24	26	29	32

their lending to Zaire, recognizing the vulnerability of the economy to declines in commodity prices. It may also reflect distrust in Zaire's ability to manage its economy, as suggested by the domestic policy indicators in Table 3.20. The persistent fiscal deficit, low or negative growth rates, and the increasing rate of inflation point to weak domestic economic management.

The unique point about Zaire is that it has had to reschedule frequently, even though the rate of increase in external debt has been comparatively low. The reschedulings, which began in early 1976, may have been a deterrent to private lenders, especially since the 1979 rescheduling was a de facto rescheduling of arrears on previously rescheduled debt (Friedman, 1984, p. 139).

Group III

In this group are developing countries that have not rescheduled, although they appear on the IMF's list of 25 major debtor nations. Countries in this group were chosen to complement a country in Groups I and II.

EGYPT

The change in the relative price of oil in the 1970s transformed Egypt's composition of exports, as is evident from Table 3.21.

Table 3.20   *Domestic Policy Indicators, Zaire*

	1973–8 (annual average)	1978–9	1979–80	1980–1	1981–2	1982–3
Real GDP growth (%) (1980 prices)	− 2.4	0.26	2.4	2.4	− 1.8	0.98

	1973–8 (annual average)	1979	1980	1981	1982	1983
Fiscal deficit as a % of GNP	12.4	4.5	1.4	5.6		
Price index (1980 prices)	14.6	70.4	100	134.9	185	326

Table 3.21   *Composition of Main Exports (Percentage of Main Export Value), 1975 and 1982, Egypt*

1975		1982	
Raw cotton	48	Crude oil	62
Cotton yarn	15	Raw cotton	14
Cotton waste and other fibres	10	Oil products	12
Crude oil and products	7	Cotton yarn	4
Rice	6	Aluminium ingots	2.3
Fruit	5	Oranges	2
Cotton fabrics	4	Potatoes	1.5
Iron and steel	2.5	Cotton and woven goods	1.5
Onions	2.1	Bleached rice	0.3
Potatoes	0.76		

Source: EIU, *Quarterly Economic Review of Egypt* Annual Supplements 1975 and 1982.

As Table 3.21 illustrates, the composition of Egypt's exports has changed since the mid-1970s. Crude oil is now the primary source of export revenue, and cotton-related exports have declined in importance. This profile is similar to Mexico's, although Egypt's exports are considerably more diversified. In Egypt, agricultural products continue to make a contribution to export earnings, but they have become a minor contributor in Mexico. The greater diversification in Egypt means that the country is less subject to world price shocks, oil being the most obvious case.

Turning to Egypt's external indicators (Table 3.22), we see that the figures are more stable than for Mexico. A rising current account deficit has been balanced by inflows of capital, with a smooth appreciation of the value of the currency against the SDR.

Egypt's external debt figures, in Table 3.23, indicate a number of important differences from the Mexican case.

Table 3.22   *External Indicators, Egypt*

	1973–8 (annual average)	1979	1980	1981	1982	1983
£E/SDRs	0.47	0.90	0.91	0.83	0.73	0.75
Current account ($bn)	− 0.7	− 1.51	− 0.44	− 2.1	− 2.2	
Capital account ($bn)	0.74	1.6	1.1	2.2	2.3	
Terms of trade	NA					

Table 3.23   *External Debt, Egypt*

	1973	1975	1977	1978	1979	1980	1981	1982
DOD ($bn)	2.2	4.9	8.1	9.9	11.4	12.8	14.25	14.94
of which: (%)								
Official creditors	74	81	84	86	84	84	80	80
Private creditors	26	19	16	14	16	16	20	20
VIL (%)	—	4.2	5.7	5.1	4.6	3.8	3.3	2
Con.L (%)	58	74.4	76.7	76.5	74.6	74.4	71.2	70.6

The average annual growth rate in external debt for Egypt was approximately 21 per cent; the same figure for Mexico is marginally higher at 25 per cent. If the two debt tables are compared, it is seen that the proportion of disbursed debt subject to variable rates of interest and concessional rates of interest are inversed for Egypt. The fact that such a small proportion of Egypt's debt is subject to variable rates of interest insulated debt-servicing from the interest rate shock.

In terms of domestic policy indicators, Egypt has controlled inflation more successfully than Mexico, though the size of Egypt's deficit as a percentage of GNP has been, on average, higher than for Mexico (see Table 3.24). Egypt does not appear to have experienced Mexico's

Table 3.24   *Domestic Policy Indicators, Egypt*

	1973–8 (annual average)	1978–9	1981–2
Real GDP growth (%) (1980 prices)	8.9	8.7	5.5

	1973–8 (annual average)	1979	1980	1981	1982	1983
Price index (1980 = 100)	58.8	82.9	100	110	127	147

	1975–8 (annual average)	1979	1980	1981	1982	1983
Deficit as a % of GDP	16	14	NA	6	16	12

Table 3.25   Composition of Main Exports (Percentage of Main Export Value), 1974–5 and 1982–3, India

1974–5		1982–3	
Engineering goods	14.6	Handicrafts	21
Sugar	14	Engineering goods	14
Jute manufactures	12	Cotton apparel	9.4
Tea	9.3	Iron ore	6.7
Handicrafts	8	Tea	6.5
Iron ore	6.6	Fish and fish preparations	6.2
Cotton fabrics	6.5	Leather and leather	
Leather and leather		manufactures	6.2
manufactures (excluding		Chemicals	5.5
footwear)	6	Cotton fabrics	4.7
Cashew kernels	5	Tobacco	4.3
Oil cakes	4	Jute manufactures	3.6
Cotton apparel	4	Coffee	3.3
Chemical and allied products	3.8	Oil cakes	2.7
Tobacco	3.4	Cashew kernels	2.4
Fish and fish preparations	3	Sugar	1.8
Iron and steel	0.86	Spices	1.6
		Iron and steel	0.99

Source: EIU, Quarterly Economic Review of India Annual Supplements 1977 and 1984.

decline in real growth rates from 1981 onwards, although a rather critical period, 1979–80 and 1980–1, has had to be left out because Egypt's GDP for 1980 is not available. The comparatively good performance of Egypt's GDP growth rate suggests that the impact of the world recession did not hit Egypt as hard as Mexico, probably owing to the diversified nature of Egypt's economy.

INDIA

India is classified as a 'low income' country by the IMF subgrouping of non oil developing countries. India did reschedule during the period 1975 to 1980, but this was part of an aid consortia agreement and, as such, does not represent a true rescheduling of sovereign debt.

The diversified nature of India's exports is illustrated in Table 3.25. It means that the country is less subject to random fluctuations in earnings as the world economy moves in and out of recession. The comparatively low percentage of primary commodities also protects India from their price volatility. There have not been any major changes in the composition of exports, with the possible exception of

Table 3.26   *External Indicators, India*

	1973–8 (annual average)	1979	1980	1981	1982	1983
Rupees/SDRs	10.0	10.5	10.2	10.2	10.4	10.8
Current account ($mn)	813	50	− 1,785	− 2,698		
Capital account ($mn)	442	488	1,183	850		
Terms of trade (1980 = 100)	120	108	100			

the decline in importance of jute manufactures and the increased percentage contribution made by handicrafts. India is vulnerable on the import side to fluctuations in oil prices. In 1974–5 the import of petroleum and petroleum products contributed to (in value terms) 28 per cent of India's main imports. This figure had risen to 39 per cent by 1982–3.

India's external indicators are summarized in Table 3.26. It is notable that the rupee/SDR exchange rate has hardly moved through the period 1973 to 1983. Unfortunately, the dated terms of trade information make it difficult to assess what the correct movement of the exchange rate should be, although the deterioration of the TOT through to 1980 does not appear to be registering in the value of the currency.

Table 3.27 provides information on India's external debt situation. The average annual growth rate in public or publicly guaranteed disbursed debt outstanding was approximately 6 per cent (in nominal terms) over the period 1973 to 1982, far lower than the growth rates of this debt for the countries reviewed to date. While India's debt almost doubled over the period, Zaire's experienced a fourfold increase.

Table 3.27   *External Debt, India*

	1973	1975	1977	1978	1979	1980	1981	1982
DOD ($bn)	10.4	12.2	14.6	15.4	15.8	17.6	18	19.6
of which: (%)								
Official creditors	97	98	98	98	98	97	96	94
Private creditors	3	2	2	2	2	3	4	6
VIL (%)	—	—	0.3	0.4	0.7	1.8	3.2	4.3
Con.L (%)	89	91	92	92	92	91	88	85

Table 3.28   *Domestic Policy Indicators, India*

	1973–8 (annual average)	1978–9	1979–80	1980–1	1981–2	
Real GDP growth (%) (1980 prices)	5.1	− 5.2	6.8	5.9	2.5	

	1973–8 (annual average)	1979	1980	1981	1982	1983
Price index (1980 = 100)	77.3	89.7	100	113	122	136

	1974–8 (annual average)	1979	1980	1981	1982
Deficit as a % of GNP	4.7	6	7	6	6.5

Compared with all the other countries reviewed, India has the most favourable debt position, with virtually none of its sovereign debt subject to variable rates of interest. India, therefore, was exempt from the real interest rate shock.

India's domestic policy indicators are summarized in Table 3.28. India has recorded a healthy real GDP growth rate from 1979 onwards, despite the world recession. The rate of increase in inflation is on the high side but is low compared with the other 'low income'

Table 3.29   *Composition of Main Exports (Percentage of Main Export Value), 1977 and 1983, Thailand*

1977		1983	
Rice	27	Rice	30
Maize	26	Tapioca products	23
Tapioca products	20.6	Rubber	17.5
Rubber	16	Maize	12.6
Tin	10.4	Sugar	9.4
		Tin metal	7.8

Source: EIU, *Quarterly Economic Review of Thailand* Annual Supplements 1977 and 1984.

country, Zaire. Deficits as a percentage of GNP have remained steady throughout the period.

THAILAND

Thailand, like Turkey, is a non oil developing country exporter of primary products. Both are in the IMF's group of 25 major debtor nations, but Thailand has no history of rescheduling. Table 3.29 illustrates Thailand's dependence on primary commodity exports.

With the exception of tin, agricultural products make up Thailand's main exports. More than 50 per cent of the main exports could be classified as staple necessities, the consumption of which is unlikely to be affected by declines in world income. On the other hand, revenues could be badly affected by weather shocks which destroy crops. In 1975, imports of fuels and lubricants made up 25 per cent of the value of Thailand's main imports; this had risen moderately to 29 per cent by 1983. Machinery, chemicals and manufactured goods are the other major contributors to Thailand's import bill. The slight increase in the value contribution of fuels indicates that Thailand has adjusted well to the oil price shocks.

Thailand's external indicators are summarized in Table 3.30. As for India, the exchange rate has remained more or less unchanged, even though the terms of trade have moved against Thailand. The current account shows a steady deficit throughout the last decade, compensated for by capital inflows.

As Table 3.31 shows, Thailand's rate of growth in external debt has been at an average annual rate of 30 per cent, which is higher than either Mexico's or Brazil's. The figures reveal that it has grown at a particularly rapid rate since 1979. The grace period for this debt averages around five years, so it may be too early to judge whether this growth rate will prove detrimental to the country's debt-servicing ability.

Table 3.30 *External Indicators, Thailand*

	1973–8 (annual average)	1979	1980	1981	1982	1983
Baht/SDRs	24.4	26.4	26.7	25.7	25.4	24.6
Current account ($bn)	− 0.58	− 2.1	− 2.1	− 2.6	− 1.0	
Capital account ($bn)	0.71	2.0	2.1	2.5	1.5	
Terms of trade (1980 = 100)	86	100	87.4	74.4	82	

Table 3.31   *External Debt, Thailand*

	1973	1975	1977	1978	1979	1980	1981	1982
DOD ($bn)	0.44	0.62	1.1	1.82	2.83	4.1	5.2	6.21
of which:								
(%)								
Official creditors	92	90	80	69	59	56	55	56
Private creditors	8	10	20	31	41	44	45	44
VIL (%)	—	2.7	12.7	18	23	29	33	31
Con.L (%)	32.4	32.4	32	30	25	24	21.5	20

The figures on external debt also indicate that Thailand is in the middle range when it comes to the proportion of DOD subject to variable rates of interest. The high real interest rates will have had an impact in Thailand, but not to the extent of some of the other debtor countries that have been reviewed.

On the domestic front, Thailand has experienced a healthy growth rate in real GDP throughout the period. The rise in the inflation rate since 1980 has been one of the lowest of all the countries reviewed. The size of the deficit as a percentage of GDP has been a steady 3–4 per cent, with the exception of 1982 when there was a slight rise.

ISRAEL AND THE REPUBLIC OF KOREA

Israel and the Republic of Korea (hereafter Korea) are classified as major exporters of manufactures in the non oil developing country

Table 3.32   *Domestic Policy Indicators, Thailand*

	1973–8 (annual average)	1978–9	1979–80	1980–1	1981–2	1982–3
Real GDP growth (%) (1980 = 100)	7.7	6	5.8	6.3	4.1	5.8

	1975–8 (annual average)	1979	1980	1981	1982	1983
Price index (1980 = 100)	66.3	84	100	112.7	118.6	123
Deficit as a % of GNP	2.4	3.8	4.7	3.5	5.9	4.1

Table 3.33   *Composition of Main Exports (Percentage of Main Export Value), 1974 and 1983, Israel*

1974		1983	
Polished diamonds	43	Agricultural exports	10
Chemicals	15	Industrial exports	90
Textiles, clothing, leather	11		
Citrus fruit	8.2		
Foodstuffs	8		
Mining products	6.1		
Other fruit and vegetables	3.2		
Rubber and plastics	2.5		
Fresh fruit and vegetables	1.6		

Source: EIU, *Quarterly Economic Review of Israel* Annual Supplements 1974 and 1984.

group. They are also on the IMF's list of 25 major debtor countries. Yet neither country has rescheduled its external debt. Each country is considered in turn.

ISRAEL

Table 3.33 illustrates the importance of industrial exports as a contributor to export revenue in Israel. In 1983, diamonds, chemicals and textiles were the main components of industrial exports. Agricultural exports have declined in relative importance since 1975. Compared to Brazil, Israel's fuel imports are not as much a contributor to the import bill, accounting for 18.7 per cent of the total value of imports in 1983.

Turning to Israel's external indicators (Table 3.34), we see a rapid and significant devaluation in the value of the shekel against the SDR

Table 3.34   *External Indicators, Israel*

	1973–8 (annual average)	1979	1980	1981	1982	1983
Shekels/SDR	1.0	3.3	6.7	13.5	26.8	60.1
Current account ($bn)	− 0.96	− 0.86	− 0.81	− 1.43	− 2.2	− 2.2
Capital account ($bn)	− 1.1	− 1.75	− 1.2	− 2.06	− 2.8	− 1.7
Terms of trade (1980 = 100)	109.7	109	100	99.8	103	105

Table 3.35   *External Debt, Israel*

	1973	1975	1977	1978	1979	1980	1981	1982
DOD ($bn)	4.5	5.92	8.1	9.2	10.3	12.6	14.3	14.9
of which:								
(%)								
Official creditors	48	53	59	62	69	70	68	69
Private creditors	52	47	41	38	31	30	32	31
VIL (%)	—	—	1.2	2.0	2.7	5.8	6.3	6.4
Con.L (%)	41	47	54	58	59	51	43	39

from 1979 and especially after 1983. There is a steady improvement in Israel's terms of trade after 1981.

The external debt figures for Israel (Table 3.35) show that the proportion of debt subject to variable rates of interest is small. The majority of the public or publicly guaranteed external DOD was loaned to Israel by official creditors, private creditors accounting for just under one-third of the total. Israel's average annual growth rate of external debt between 1973 and 1982 was lower than for most of the countries reviewed here, at 12.7 per cent.

The domestic policy indicators are the worst for all the economies presented, as Table 3.36 illustrates. Although Israel has managed to

Table 3.36   *Domestic Policy Indicators, Israel*

	1975–8 (annual average)	1978–9	1979–80	1980–1	1981–2	1982–3
Real GDP growth (%) (1980 prices)	1.7	3.7	2.65	2.8	1.045	1.8

	1975–9 (annual average)	1980	1981	1982	1983
Price index (1980 = 100)	21	100	216.8	477.8	1173.5

	1974–9 (annual average)	1980	1981	1982	1983
Deficit as a % of GNP	18	15.2	19	25	24

Table 3.37 *Composition of Main Exports (Percentage of Main Export Value), 1976 and 1983, Korea*

1976		1983	
Metal manufactures	29	Machinery and transport	
Motor cars	25	equipment	43
Ships	19.5	Manufactured goods	38.3
Textiles and textile products	11.6	Miscellaneous manufactures	10.2
Chemicals	10.3	Food/live animals	6
Non-metallic minerals	2.5	Inedible raw materials	1.6
Foodstuffs	2.4	Tobacco	0.58

Source: EIU, *Quarterly Economic Review of Korea* Annual Supplements 1981 and 1984.

maintain a positive real rate of GDP growth, the size of the deficit as a percentage of GNP has been high throughout the period, reaching a peak in 1981. Inflation has been rising at an annual rate of 185 per cent since 1980.

The domestic policy track record for Israel is far worse than for Brazil and, like Brazil, Israel has been subject to the oil shock via its import bill, although not to the same degree. The exports of both countries were affected by the world recession in much the same way. The only major difference is with respect to the interest rate shock: Israel was largely protected from this. Also, Israel's growth rate in debt has not been as high: 12.7 per cent compared with Brazil's average annual growth rate of 20 per cent.

KOREA

Korea depends heavily on the export of manufactured goods, as Table 3.37 illustrates.

The contribution made by fuel to the Korean import bill has declined significantly since 1976, when the import of crude oil was responsible for 40 per cent of the value of Korea's main imports. By 1983, this figure had declined to 11 per cent. No other net oil importing developing country reviewed has made an adjustment of this size.

Examining the external indicators for Korea (Table 3.38), we find depreciation in the value of the won against the SDR throughout the period and a steady improvement in the country's terms of trade since 1980.

Table 3.39 reports Korea's external debt figures. Between 1973 and 1982, DOD grew at an annual average rate of 19 per cent. The proportion of the loans made by official creditors was just over 50 per

Table 3.38   *External Indicators, Korea*

	1973–8 (annual average)	1979	1980	1981	1982	1983
Won/SDR	451	625	750.6	803	807.2	829.3
Current account ($bn)	− 0.932	− 4.2	− 5.3	− 4.6	− 2.7	− 1.6
Capital account ($bn)	1.7	5.4	5.97	4.7	3.96	2.35
Terms of trade (1980 = 100)	108	115.3	100	113.7	119	126

cent in 1973 and in 1982 stood at 42 per cent. This indicates a gradual increase in the proportion of external loans being granted by private creditors. The percentage of loans subject to variable rates of interest was also fairly high (though not as high as Brazil's 70 per cent) by 1982 and has been rising steadily throughout the decade.

Korea's domestic indicators, presented in Table 3.40, are indicative of sound economic management. After a negative real rate of growth in 1979, the Korean economy has shown a marked recovery. Compared with other developing countries, the rise in the price index is not very high (4.5 per cent in 1982–3) and the trend of fiscal deficits is downward. Even when this peaked in 1982, it was still a relatively small percentage.

SUMMARY OF COUNTRY CASES

The objective of this section in Chapter 3 has been to apply the general model to individual country cases. Twelve countries have been chosen from the IMF's group of 25 major debtor countries. Seven of the twelve countries have had to reschedule their sovereign debt in the recent past; the other five countries were chosen because they

Table 3.39   *External Debt, Korea*

	1973	1975	1977	1978	1979	1980	1981	1982
DOD ($bn) of which: (%)	3.52	5.5	8.6	11.2	13.7	15.8	18.3	20.06
Official creditors	52	48	48	45	42	41	41	42
Private creditors	48	52	52	55	58	59	59	58
VIL (%)	8.7	21	23	21	28	29	38	41
Con.L (%)	42	31	26	23	19	18	16	14

Table 3.40   *Domestic Policy Indicators, Korea*

	1973–8 (annual average)	1978–9	1979–80	1980–1	1981–2	1982–3
Real GDP growth (%) (1980 prices)	9.8	7.3	− 3.0	6.9	5.5	9.3

	1976–8 (annual average)	1979	1980	1981	1982	1983
Price index (1980 = 100)	58.4	77.7	100	121.3	130.1	134.5

	1974–8 (annual average)	1979	1980	1981	1982	1983
Deficit as a % of GNP	1.6	1.7	2.3	3.5	3.9	1.14

had an IMF developing country status similar to at least one of the rescheduling nations.

The review of these countries lends support to the broader framework for sovereign risk analysis developed earlier in this chapter. Random shocks to the world economy had an important impact on the ability of certain nations to service their debt, although the extent of influence of each of the shocks varied with each country, depending on the export/import composition of each of the countries and on the proportion of a nation's sovereign debt subject to variable rates of interest. For example, those countries whose export revenues were dependent upon one or two primary commodities were most vulnerable to the variation in primary commodity prices. Also, while some nations (for example, India, Israel) were largely protected from the interest rate shock, other countries such as Mexico and Brazil found it increasingly difficult to service their external debt because a large proportion of their debt was subject to a variable rate of interest.

However, the complexities of identifying problem debtor countries are made apparent when we look at domestic economic policy indicators as a proxy for the social welfare function of the country. Israel has avoided rescheduling, even though it has an appalling track-record on the policy front. On the other hand, Turkey paid the price for adopting a policy of protecting the economy from the oil price increases of the 1970s and incurring a high proportion of short-term debt through the Convertible Turkish Lire Deposits.

The review of the country cases points to the secondary role played by ratio analysis on the demand side of the model. These ratios are only useful to the extent that they act as indicators of underlying problems related to shocks to the world economy and domestic policies.

One final point needs to be stressed in this summary. The review of the country cases has tended to mask the importance of events on the supply side of the general model, which were discussed earlier (see pp. 78–82). For reasons identified earlier in this chapter and in Chapter 1, the analyst can ill afford to ignore the supply side in sovereign risk assessment. This point is followed up in Chapter 4.

Conclusions: Lessons for the Sovereign Risk Analyst

Chapter 3 began with the presentation of a model of sovereign risk analysis. The approach differed from those reviewed in Chapter 2 mainly because it included a full specification of the economic determinants of the demand and supply of sovereign loans. The probability of default equation emerged as an endogenous part of a more general system, where default was defined as either a temporary suspension of payments or outright repudiation.

On the demand side, the most important factors influencing a change in the probability of default were:

(1)   Random shocks, which reduce the size of the variable (s) that the national government is trying to maximize. For example, if GNP is the welfare objective and random shocks, either directly or indirectly, lower GNP, then default is more likely.

(2)   The way the social welfare function of the borrowing country was defined. A government with a welfare objective of short-run consumption per head as opposed to long-run growth objectives would be more likely to default.

(3)   The degree of borrower risk aversion to reductions in the country's welfare objective.

On the supply side, increases in lender risk aversion to either type of default and reductions in First World wealth could have important negative influences on the supply of sovereign credit.

The general framework for sovereign risk analysis developed in the first section in this chapter was applied to the current situation in the next section. After a review at the international level, data on a number of selected countries were scrutinized with the objective of assessing how well events in these countries fit into the general framework. As this review illustrated, many of the rescheduling problems were explained by this general model. Countries vulnerable to the shocks of world recession, higher interest rates and fluctuations in commodity prices tended to reschedule, especially if domestic policy indicators pointed to a myopic welfare objective.

There are three lessons for the sovereign risk analyst. First, it is essential to be familiar with the domestic economic policy record of individual sovereign borrowers. This permits the analyst to assess the welfare objectives of the country. Secondly, the analyst must be aware of the vulnerability of the economy of the sovereign borrower to shocks in the international economy. In particular, the analyst should identify the main components of export revenue and the import bill, the terms on which a nation's sovereign debt position has been negotiated, and the flow of capital into the country in relation to its current account position. Changing patterns in the world economy must also be part of the analyst's brief, including the supply side of the international capital markets. Little will be achieved by the observation of a few debt-related ratios at the expense of these other important factors. In Chapter 4, the implications of these two lessons are further expanded by reviewing the ideal components of a country spread sheet and report.

The third and final lesson relates to the recognition by all sovereign lenders of the unique aspects of this type of loan. Its 'sovereign' nature differentiates the loan from the other loans in a bank's portfolio. This is also the underlying reason for third party (mainly IMF) intervention, which has been characteristic of the rescheduling packages. Third party intervention of this sort is not easily modelled in the general framework developed in this chapter. None the less it is vitally important that the sovereign risk analyst understands the issues arising from the interdependent nature of sovereign lending. These are discussed in Chapter 5.

Notes: Chapter 3

1. For example, the Kletzer supply side assumes that each risk neutral lender seeks to maximize expected profit in terms of the amount loaned to

sovereign nations. As the reader will come to observe, the assumptions made on the supply side in this chapter are quite different.

2. The original presentations of the state preference theory may be found in Debreu, 1959, and in Arrow, 1964. Hirshleifer, 1965, and Green, 1976 (ch. 15), provide good interpretations of the state preference approach.

3. The proof for condition (1) may be found in Markowitz, 1959; Feldstein, 1969, provides the proof for condition (2).

4. The discussion of the influence of the explanatory variables is based on knowledge of each of the coefficients, the details of which may be found in Heffernan, 1985. Readers should not be distressed if they find the commentary does not follow immediately from the system of equations. The latter was presented to provide readers with an idea of the type of equations that result from using the general framework and, for this reason, the technical detail on the equations was omitted.

5. A model developed by G. E. Feder and K. Ross for the Swiss Banking Corporation suggests that, up to the end of 1982, risk neutrality best described the behaviour of the banks in their decision to make sovereign loans but, since this date, risk aversion has been a better description. See the report by T. Povey in *The Financial Times*, 'World Banking Survey', part 1, 9 May 1983, p. 9.

6. The large percentage of official credit and relatively low proportion of loans subject to variable rates of interest is partly explained by US aid (military and otherwise) granted to Turkey because of its strategic importance. Similar remarks apply in the cases of Israel, Egypt and, to a lesser extent, Korea.

4 Writing a Country Report

This chapter is concerned with the question of how the sovereign risk analyst should write a country report. It is assumed that this report is going to a credit committee, which will decide whether a sovereign loan should be granted to a country or sovereign loan exposure in a developing nation should be increased. The credit committee will need different information to answer these questions. The country report should be an important part of the information in relation to either question. However, the final decision by the credit committee will need to include considerations other than the country report. For example, if the credit committee is considering a sovereign loan for a developing country with a growth potential based on the successful production of a primary product, the bank will not wish to be involved in a high exposure to the country if a substantial part of the existing loan portfolio consists of loans to domestic firms which produce the same commodity. The decision should also be taken with the knowledge that, if the country encounters debt-servicing problems, involvement of other lenders and IMF intervention is likely, thereby diluting the power of the individual bank in its negotiations with the borrower. This problem receives a good deal of attention in Chapter 5.

The point to be made here is that the credit committee must view the decision to invest in this type of risky asset from a very broad perspective. The job of the country report writer is to submit an informed report which will help the credit committee to achieve this goal. The chapter is divided into three sections: first, a review of the use of a country spread sheet; secondly, an examination of the written part of the country report; thirdly, a conclusion, with some advice for the credit committee.

The Country Spread Sheet

Most banks exposed in sovereign lending ask their country report writers to produce a 'country spread sheet' on the borrowing country and a written summary of the economic environment of the country in question. The components of the spread sheet vary from bank to bank, but one typical of the type used is shown in Figure 4.1. This is

Figure 4.1 A 'typical' country spread sheet

NAME OF COUNTRY

	Annual Figures				Quarterly Figures			
Currency US$ Billion								
A. DOMESTIC ECONOMIC INDICATORS								
1. Size of Economy								
1.1. Population (millions)								
1.2. Population Growth (%)								
1.3. GDP ($ billions)								
1.4. GDP per head ($)								
2. Growth of Economy (at Constant Prices)								
2.1. GDP Growth % p.a.								
2.2. GDP per head growth % p.a.								
2.3. Unemployment (%)								
3. Inflationary Indicators								
3.1. Consumer Price Index Growth % p.a.								
3.2. Money Supply Growth % p.a.								
3.3 Budget Deficit ( ) or Surplus as % of GDP								
4. Exchange Rate								
4.1. Exchange Rate to US$ (End Year)								
B. BALANCE OF PAYMENTS								
1. Export of Goods								
of which % (a)								
(b)								
(c)								
2. Import of goods								
3. TRADE BALANCE								
4. Exports of Invisibles and Services:								
5. Imports of Invisibles and Services:								
6. INVISIBLES BALANCE								
7. NET TRANSFERS								
8. CURRENT BALANCE (B3 + B6 + B7)								
9. Long Term Capital (plus Investment Flows)								
10. Short Term Capital								
11. CAPITAL ACCOUNT (B9 + B10)								
12. CURRENT AND CAPITAL BALANCE (B8 + B11)								
13. ERRORS AND OMISSIONS								
14. CHANGE IN RESERVES (B12 + B13)								

Figure 4.1 A 'typical' country spread sheet (continued)

NAME OF COUNTRY

	Annual Figures					Quarterly Figures				
Currency US$ Billion										
C. FOREIGN ASSETS (END PERIOD)										
1. International Reserves										
2. Unutilised IMF Credit										
3. Other Foreign Assets										
4. TOTAL										
D. DEBT STRUCTURE (END PERIOD)										
1. External Debt										
(a) of which Public Debt										
(b) Private Debt										
(c) and of which Under 1 Year										
(d) Over 1 Year										
3.										
4.										
E. GROSS NEW DEBT										
1. International Loans – Public										
2. – Private										
3. TOTAL										
F. DEBT INDICATORS										
1. Debt Service Payments										
2. Total Exports (B1 + B4)										
3. Debt Service Ratio (F1 × 100 + F2)										
4. Debt % GDP (D1 × 100 + A1.3)										
5. Debt % Exports (D1 × 100 + F2)										
6. Foreign Assets % External Debt (C5 × 100 + D1)										
7. ditto % Short Term Debt (C5 × 100 + D1c)										
8. ditto % Imports (C5 × 100 + (B2 + B5))										

currently being employed by a London-based international bank involved in sovereign lending. The bank kindly agreed to submit the spread sheet for critical review. For obvious reasons, it has chosen to remain anonymous.

Figure 4.1 shows how the spread sheet is divided into six sections. In Section A, the report writer is asked to fill in information on domestic indicators. Five years of annual figures are provided, as well as quarterly data.

We must begin by asking why this selection of quarterly and annual data is chosen. Identifying trends in economic policy is difficult if we are relying upon a five-year interval and/or quarterly data. Of course, it depends where this spread sheet fits into the report-writing process. If it is an annual update of figures, which has been done for at least a decade and filed, it is acceptable to report with a five-year or even two-year dating. The credit committee and report writer can always refer to earlier spread sheets. However, it will still be the job of the report writer to note any changes in trends. This would not be possible if we relied solely on a five-year period. If the country is being reviewed for the first time, then a more extensive presentation of figures will be necessary and this will form the basis for future annual reports. Countries to which sovereign loans have been made in the past should receive an annual review of the figures. In a relatively short period of time, the bank will have acquired a very good data base. In some banks, the spread sheets and country report writing is done on an ad hoc basis, when the credit committee requests a report. This is a mistake, because the lack of a systematic approach makes it more difficult to identify deviations in economic trends, which should be one of the primary purposes of report writing.

Turning to the individual items reported in Figure 4.1, A, we can see it is divided into three subsections. The report writer is asked to complete information on the size of the economy, the real growth rate of the economy and inflationary indicators. Some of these figures are unnecessary. The purpose of the domestic indicators should be to convey information on domestic economic policy. For example, what is the welfare objective (discussed in Chapter 3) of the country? A direct answer cannot be given to this question, but it is important because it is likely that a government concerned with maximizing consumption per head or short-term national income is more likely to opt for an inflationary growth policy than a country with long-term income maximizing objectives.

To obtain some indication of domestic policy objectives, the following data should be included:

(1) Real GDP growth rates.

(2) GDP per capita.

(3) Share of investment in national income.

(4) Consumer price index.

(5) Deficit as a percentage of GNP.

(6) Unemployment rates.

The first two of these indicators provide information on how fast the economy and per capita incomes are growing. There is no point in including nominal figures on either absolute GDP or its rate of growth. These figures will mean little to individuals lacking an intimate knowledge of the economy and, in an inflationary environment, they provide no indication of domestic policy management or the general health of the economy. The rate of increase in per capita income will yield information on how well the population is doing in terms of increases in standard of living.

The share of investment in national income is measured by taking the annual figures for gross fixed capital formation and dividing this by the country's gross national product. In Chapter 1 it was pointed out that, for non oil developing countries taken as a whole, this figure rose steadily throughout the 1970s, suggesting that external capital was being used for investment rather than for consumption purposes. If this figure is tracked over time for individual countries, we are able to judge whether investment as a share of national income is steady throughout the period. A country with a declining share must be a source of concern, because this means that the external capital is not being used solely for investment purposes. Of course, it is not possible to use this figure to judge whether the investment projects chosen are the optimal ones for the country in question. Unfortunately, disaggregated data on this important question are not available, unless we can rely on informal information on the projects being financed by sovereign loans. However, this is never reported in the official statistics.

The consumer price index (CPI) provides information on the rate of inflation. Other indices, such as a wholesale price index or an industrial price index, could be reported, but the CPI includes the broadest range of goods, making its movements steadier. Reporting the money supply growth rates will not be very informative. There is considerable variation in the reliability of figures on the money supply from country to country and the inflation rate provides an indirect indication of these figures. In the report itself, the writer can note the main causes of inflation, such as excessive money supply growth rates.

By 'excessive' is meant a growth rate in the money supply that is in excess of the rate of growth in national income by a significant amount. However, this is only one potential cause of inflation; including money supply growth figures without the figures on other inflation sources may be misleading. Other causes of inflation include high wage settlements, rising capital costs and a depreciating currency.

The budget deficit as a percentage of GNP is an important indicator of the degree of expansionary fiscal policy in the economy. GNP is preferable to GDP because it is a measure of all economic activity, including that of foreign residents, and therefore will provide a better indication of the effects of expansionary policy. If these figures are unobtainable, then GDP may be used.

Finally, the unemployment rate gives a measure of the degree of excess capacity in the economy and may also provide an indicator of potential unrest if there is a rapid increase in the rate of unemployment over a number of years.

The spread sheet in Figure 4.1 includes the exchange rate as a domestic economic indicator. We can sympathise with its inclusion here, because it tends to be the case that countries in which economies follow strict aggregate demand policies are more likely to allow their currencies to depreciate than countries that follow very expansionary policies. However, it is probably best to include this indicator with the figures on the external performance of the economy, because it is difficult to judge whether an appreciating or depreciating exchange rate is appropriate without having more information on the balance of payments position.

Part B of the representative spread sheet includes extensive detail on the balance of payments. When choosing the external indicators we must ask what purpose is being served by their inclusion. For example, what information is conveyed by information on the nominal values of exports and imports of goods, services and invisible items? The primary purpose of the external indicators should be to provide an indication of how vulnerable the economy is to changes in the fortunes of the world economy. With this in mind, the section of the spread sheet on 'external indicators' (see list, p. 139) should include:

(7) A measure of the openness of the economy:

$$\frac{1}{2}(EX/GDP + IM/GDP)$$

where EX is the value of exports and IM is the value of imports. By computing this figure, we acquire information on the degree to which an economy is dependent on world trade and, therefore, is subject to shocks in the world economy. If reported over a number of years (at least a decade), it is also possible to judge whether the economy is growing more or less open with time. For example, Korea has grown more open in the last decade, moving from a figure of 33 per cent to 43 per cent, while Brazil has increased its openness from 6 per cent to 8 per cent. The figure for the United States recently reached 16 per cent.

To get a true measure of vulnerability, however, it is necessary to look at disaggregated data on exports and imports. This information is not easily included in a spread sheet, and it is probably best reported in a supplementary table. The table should include a breakdown of the composition of exports and imports of the sort reported in Chapter 3 for the individual country cases. This is extremely valuable information, because it permits us to assess the points of vulnerability of a particular economy. For example, a country relying on primary commodity exports for earnings will be subject to the tendency of commodity prices to be highly volatile and to vary directly with the state of the world economy. A country heavily dependent on energy imports will likewise be subject to volatile prices.

If export revenues or imports are relatively minor for an economy (and this will be indicated by the openness ratio) then it would be helpful to extend the supplementary table by including figures on the percentage contribution to GDP by sector.

(8)   Volume indices for exports and imports.

(9)   The terms of trade.

The volume indices abstract from the influences of price changes on the growth rate of exports and imports. This will be especially important if the value figures for exports and imports are distorted because of price volatility. Accompanying these figures should be a value index, the terms of trade. The terms of trade is the ratio of the export price index to the import price index. A TOT improvement indicates export prices have either risen more quickly or declined more slowly than import prices.

Taken together, these two indices provide valuable information on the trends in export revenues and import bill for a given country. For example, the Korean TOT moved against this economy after 1979 but the export volume index rose by almost 40 per cent compared with an increase in the import volume index of approximately 21 per cent. On the other hand, Brazil experienced a decline in its TOT of approximately the same magnitude over the period but the rate of increase in its export volume index was only 10 per cent greater than the import volume index. The implications of these two movements for the current account of the balance of payments are important.

Korea was able to avoid a serious deterioration in its current account deficit of the balance of payments during this period, whereas Brazil's deteriorated very rapidly.

If these figures are recorded over a long enough period of time (e.g. 20 years), the writer will be able to assess how well the economy adjusts to downturns in the world economy or to international shocks.

(10)   Current account of the balance of payments.

(11)   Capital account of the balance of payments.

This information will give the reader of the country spread sheet an immediate idea of whether a country's balance of payments is deteriorating or improving and, read in conjunction with the terms of trade and volume indices, will permit judgement to be made on the reasons for a worsening or improvement in the balance of payments. The spread sheet in Figure 4.1 distinguishes between short-term and long-term capital movements. This is not necessary in the external indicator section, but it should be included in the debt section. More will be said about this below. The capital account figure should exclude reserves, which should be considered separately in the debt data as an indicator of liquidity.

(12)   The exchange rate

By reporting the exchange rate after the current account and capital account figures, it is possible to judge whether the country is permitting its exchange rate to move in line with its balance of payments position or whether there is a great deal of intervention in the exchange markets to prevent the exchange rate from reflecting its true value. The real effective exchange rate would be the ideal measure. It measures the value of the currency against the weighted value of the currencies of the country's major trading partners (hence the term effective) and adjusts this for the relative rates of inflation in the home economy and in the economies of the country's trading partners (hence the term real). Unfortunately, the IMF reports this exchange rate for industrialized countries only. For developing countries, we have to use either the period average (a year if the International Financial Statistics are being used), national currency value of the SDR or of the US dollar. The SDR rate is preferable unless the country does a large percentage of its trade with the United States. A rise in either of these rates implies a depreciation in the home country currency.

Variables (7) to (12) complete the section on external indicators. Referring to Figure 4.1, this would replace section B of the spread sheet and would be accompanied by a supplement on the composition of exports and imports. This provides the assessor with information which allows him or her to judge the vulnerability of the economy to international economic problems more accurately than does the information provided on the sample spread sheet, especially items B1 to B7.

The next part of the country spread sheet in Figure 4.1 is divided into four parts: Foreign Assets (section C); Debt Structure (section D); Gross New Debt (section E); Debt Indicators (section F). Instead of reporting the related figures in separate sections, it would be more appropriate to include the figures in a 'creditworthiness' section, because this is really what these figures are trying to indicate. The section could include long-term and short-term trends: the former would concentrate on the change in certain key variables over a long period of time, while figures for the short run would indicate the current debt position. This section of the spread sheet would report the following:

(13)   The growth rate in external public or publicly guaranteed disbursed debt outstanding.

This may be obtained from the World Bank's *World Debt Tables* and is a good proxy for the amount of sovereign lending in the country. The *World Debt Tables* also include non-guaranteed external debt data for some countries. Growth rates should be reported for as long a time period as possible, with the nominal values reported for the two end years; the latter will give the analyst the size of the external debt in relation to the bank's loan portfolio. However, these rates do not need to be cited for every year, since the growth rate in external debt yields more useful information.

An alternative source is the Development Assistance Committee (DAC) of the OECD, which compiles data on the public and private external debt of developing countries. One of its main sources is the Debt Reporting System of the World Bank, but it also relies on data from the Creditor Reporting System. The latter provides information on the public debt owed to the countries of the DAC by 158 developing countries in the forms of official development assistance, other official flows, and officially guaranteed private export credits. In addition, the DAC uses data from private banks, the central banks of the debtor countries, the IMF and the Bank of International Settlements (BIS). The data are presented in OECD's *Geographical Distribution of Financial Flows to Developing Countries*, which was last published in 1984. As noted by Dennis (1984, p. 251) the DAC figures for external debt of the developing countries tend to be higher than those compiled in the World Bank's *World Debt Tables*, probably because of differences in the estimates of external debt when more than one source is being used.

Unfortunately, the World Bank and DAC data exclude short-term external debt. Information on short-term external debt is difficult to obtain, yet it can be important, as the Turkish case demonstrated. The BIS and the World Bank are working to rectify this omission in the data. In the six-monthly BIS *Press Release* on the maturity distribution of external debt owed by developing (and developed) countries to private banks, the proportion of short-term debt is reported. However, no distinction is made between sovereign and other types of external debt. The World Bank (1984) has emphasized the problems of keeping track of short-term external debt, noting that most governments (including those in industrial countries) lack adequate reporting procedures.

(14)   The percentage change in the terms of trade.
(15)   The percentage change in the London Interbank Offered Rate (LIBOR).

Tracking these two variables together permits us to assess the ability of the country to service its external debt, assuming a fairly large proportion of this is subject to variable rates of interest. The two variables will give an idea of the degree to which a country suffers from a front-loading problem, as defined in Chapter 3 (see p. 94). Front-loading results from sudden increases in nominal rates of interest, which raise the up-front payments on external debt. If the ratio of export to import prices is moving in the country's favour, the increased up-front burden is more likely to be met through higher trade revenues. On the other hand, a serious deterioration in the TOT at a time when interest rates are rising rapidly will make the servicing of debt more difficult. Unfortunately, the terms of trade cannot be computed for all countries from the IMF statistics. In these cases, the rate of change in the export value index will be a reasonably good second best. These variables will be very good at picking up short-term debt-servicing problems.

(16)   Percentage of disbursed debt subject to variable rates of interest.

In periods of volatile interest rates, this will be an important variable to consider. This point was evident in Chapter 3, when individual country cases were examined as applications of the sovereign loan model. Those countries (e.g. India and Israel) with very low proportions of external debt were protected from the important interest rate shock of the 1970s. In the case of Israel, this may explain why rescheduling of sovereign debt has not been necessary, despite poor external and domestic policy indicators.

(17)   An indicator of world liquidity.

This provides the bank with an indication of the supply side of sovereign lending and more generally international lending. It is a difficult variable to measure. The Bank of England normally provides an annual summary and discussion of the BIS, IMF and other international and lending banking statistics in the March issue of its *Quarterly Bulletin*. (See, for example, the paper, 'The international banking and capital markets in 1984', in the *Bank of England Quarterly Bulletin*, March 1985, p. 58. Among other data, the article includes growth rates of gross and net international lending.)

The BIS is the key source for information on the maturity distribution of the assets and liabilities of international banks. From the standpoint of sovereign risk, special attention must be paid to the maturity distribution of the debt owed by developing countries to the private international banks. In addition to providing information on trends in international liquidity, the degree of exposure of the private banking system is also revealed. The data may be found in the BIS *Press Release: The Maturity Distribution of International Bank Lending*, published every six months. The publication includes country data (for both developed and developing countries) on the maturity distribution (i.e. up to one year, between one and two years, and more than two years) of external claims and unused credit commitments of BIS reporting banks. However, sovereign external claims are not separated from the aggregate.

(18)   Debt related ratios.

In Chapter 2, a critical review of the statistical models of sovereign risk analysis was undertaken. Several problems with this approach were identified, one of them being multicollinearity or the lack of independence among explanatory variables. This creates problems when it actually comes to using these variables because we are unsure of their relative degree of importance. Also, the different studies have come up with a bewildering number of economic variables, identified as statistically significant in one study but not in others. None the less, several variables are common to most of the models and, provided they are treated with caution and within a much more general framework, they are of some use. The author favours the following indicators:

(18A)   The Debt Service Ratio and the Ratio of External Debt to Exports. As was noted in Chapter 2 (see p. 36), the latter ratio is an indicator of problems over a long term, while the DSR may be used to identify sudden short-term problems. All of the statistical models find at least one of these variables statistically significant and Cline (1984) finds that either ratio performs equally well. Both should be included because they provide information on different time-spans. The DSR will complement the information on movements in LIBOR and the terms of trade.

(18B)   Capital Inflows as a Percentage of Debt Service is the capital account counterpart to the DSR and, with the DSR, will help the analyst to focus on short-term debt-servicing difficulties. This ratio is preferable to providing information on short-term and long-term capital inflows that do not directly relate to the debt-servicing requirements of the country.

(18C)   The Ratio of Reserves of a Country to its Imports of goods and services provides an indication of short-term liquidity problems. If a sudden drop in the ratio is observed, the analyst has to question the reasons for this. The ratio may be cited either in terms of numbers of months or as a percentage.

The reader will note the small selecton of ratio indicators in comparison with all the ones cited in statistical studies. As has been stressed at several points, these ratios should be used in conjunction with a much broader study; tracking a large variety of them will not be any more productive than following the four ratios cited, all of which provide the analyst with a different piece of information.

(18D)   If analysts are determined to employ a statistical model in the country spread sheet, the P scores produced by the Taffler and Abassi Study (1982) may be a useful way of summarizing the results of a statistical model. As was noted in Chapter 2, the Taffler and Abassi model of discriminant analysis is one of the most sophisticated of those available, with a good deal of attention devoted to the problem of multicollinearity. This model has since been developed and extended by the International Economic Appraisal service of the Economist Intelligence Unit. The P scores are percentile versions of the country Z scores (see Chapter 2, p. 45) and, as such, they permit comparison from one year to the next and also across countries. A falling P score for a given country could signal to the bank that further investigation of the sources of the country's economic problems are necessary. The P score is a compact and efficient way of getting the most out of a statistical model while keeping sovereign risk analysis within a much broader framework.

This completes the section on the ideal figures that should be included on a country spread sheet. They are summarized in Figure 4.2, with the data sources for the indicators. In the next section, the ideal written report to accompany the spread sheet is discussed.

Figure 4.2   The ideal country spread sheet

A.   DOMESTIC POLICY INDICATORS

---

1.   Real GDP Growth Rates: The International Monetary Fund's *International Financial Statistics* (hereafter, IFS) publishes the real GDP figures for member countries. It is published every quarter with an annual update in the *Yearbook*. From this it is possible to compute the growth rate in real GDP.

---

2.   GDP per capita: Available from the same source as 1.

---

3.   Investment as a Share in National Income: The IFS reports figures on Gross Fixed Capital Formation and Gross National Product. The ratio of these figures provide the percentage share of investment in national income. For some countries, Gross Capital Formation figures are reported instead of Gross Fixed Capital Formation. The former includes inventories and the latter excludes them. Either figure can be used, but Gross Fixed is the better of the two.

---

4.   Consumer Price Index: IFS.

---

5.   Deficit as a percentage of GNP: Figures for a country's nominal GNP may be found in the IFS. The best figures on the deficit position of the central government of a country may be found in the relevant country summary table of the IMF publication, *Government Finance Statistics Yearbook*.

---

6.   Unemployment Rate: It may not be possible to obtain information on this figure for some developing countries. The best data source is the *International Labour Organization Yearbook*.

B.   EXTERNAL INDICATORS

---

7.   The Openness Measure: The IMF's IFS provides the data necessary for this computation. The best source for the supplement on the main components of a country's exports and imports are the Annual Country Reports published by the *Economist* Intelligence Unit (EIU). The United Nations *Yearbook of International Trade Statistics*, vol. 1, also provides the components of international trade for each country, but the information is dated. For example, the 1982 *Yearbook* was published in 1984.

Figure 4.2   The ideal country spread sheet (continued)

8.   Volume Indices for Exports and Imports: Available from the IMF's IFS. Unfortunately, the data are incomplete for some countries.

9.   Terms of Trade: May be computed by dividing the index for the unit value of exports by the unit value of imports index. These are available in the IFS publication, but like variable 8 there are gaps in the data for some countries.

10.   Current Account: Provided by the IFS publication.

11.   Capital Account excluding reserves: As in 10.

12.   Exchange rate: As in 11.

C.   DATA ON EXTERNAL DEBT

13.   Growth Rate in Nominal Public or Publicly Guaranteed Disbursed Debt Outstanding: The absolute values for these figures are reported in the World Bank's *World Debt Tables* (WDT). An alternative source is the OECD's *Geographical Distribution of Financial Flows to Developing Countries*, 1984, although it is not published on an annual basis.

14.   Percentage change in terms of trade: From the Terms of Trade figures computed in 9.

15.   Percentage Change in LIBOR: The IFS provide a table on international interest rates, from which rates of change in LIBOR may be computed.

16.   Proportion of a Country's Disbursed Debt Outstanding (subject to variable rates of interest): From the WDT.

17.   World Liquidity: *The Bank of England Quarterly Bulletin* and BIS *Press Release: The Maturity Distribution of International Bank Lending.*

18.   Ratios:

A.   DSR and D/Exports: Available from the country tables in the WDT.

B.   Capital Inflows/Debt Service: Capital Inflows (Direct and Other Long-Term Capital) are reported for each country in the IMF's *Balance of Payments Statistics Yearbook*. Debt service data are available from the WDT.

C.   Reserves/Imports of Goods and Services: From the relevant country table of the WDT.

D.   *P* scores: Country *P* scores may be obtained from the International Economic Appraisal Service of the EIU.

The Written Report

Quality and brevity are the key words in the vocabulary of the country report writer. Members of the credit committee will be hard pressed to invest the time in reading a long-winded report. Nor need the report be long: six to eight pages should be sufficient, depending on whether a country is going through a difficult economic time and assuming that these reports are updated on an annual if not semi-annual basis.

The country report should be divided into three sections and should utilize data provided by the spread sheet. Domestic policy trends would be reviewed in section 1, followed by external indicators in section 2. In section 3, the trends in creditworthiness should be discussed.

The discussion of the ideal spread sheet was deliberately vague about the dates for which most of the data will be reported. This is because they will vary, depending on the purpose of the country report. If a bank is considering a loan to a country for the first time the main concern will be with long-term trends, whereas an annual update in a country report will concentrate on what has happened in the country since the previous report. The same distinction will apply to the written part of the report.

The written report needs to concentrate on three issues. On the domestic policy front, the report writer should indicate to the committee the type of domestic economic policy to which the government of the country is committed. If the report is being submitted for the first time, the historical trends in the country in relation to domestic economic policy should be discussed. For example, governments in the South East Asian nations have typically been committed to policies of export-led growth as a means of maximizing the welfare of their citizens. On the other hand, many Latin American countries have tended to follow policies of import substitution. The problem with the latter approach is the distorting effects of protectionist policies on the development of an economy, which in turn may affect the ability of a country to remain creditworthy.

Countries with traditionally high fiscal deficits as a percentage of GNP and or unacceptably high inflation rates provide important signals to the potential lender. If the country has been unable to show discipline in its domestic economic management, the lender should be concerned about whether a sovereign loan will be applied to a profitable investment project.

At this point in the report, it may be appropriate to comment on the political situation of the country in question. However, this part should be brief, given that the objective of the report is to provide information on the creditworthiness of a country and its ability to repay its external debt. Unless the economy is paralysed as a result of political upheaval, the political situation will have little bearing on the ability of a country to meet its external obligations. However, for a lender who has already committed sovereign funds, there is little constructive action that can be taken, even if outright repudiation of the debt is threatened. Hence, it is not worth filling up the report with a political analysis. On the other hand, if the country is being assessed for the first time, the political situation should receive more detailed attention, especially if the country has a history of political instability that has led to outright repudiation of external debt obligations. In this case, the report writer should review past political events with the objective of assessing how the country's social welfare function has influenced its ability and willingness to meet its external debt obligations.

If the country report is being written because the bank has a large number of loans made directly to firms in the country, then the influence of the political environment on the ability of these firms to repay their debt should be noted. For example, the likelihood of exchange controls or restrictions on foreign firms operating in the country should be considered. But generally a country report is not being written with this type of loan in mind.

The second part of the report, dealing with external indicators, would concentrate on the vulnerability of the economy to random shocks. The 1970s and early part of the 1980s provide good examples of how a number of random shocks can seriously undermine the ability of a country to service its external debt. Using the external indicators on the country spread sheet and the terms of the sovereign debt obligations found in part C of the spread sheet (i.e. the proportion of loans subject to variable rates of interest), the written report should identify the vulnerable points of the economy in question and then report on any world variables that might create a crisis situation for the economy of some developing countries. Some economies are inherently more subject to shocks because of the lack of economic diversification, which typifies many nations in the developing country group. However, there is a good side to all this. Over time, many of the negative random shocks will be replaced by their positive counterparts. Primary commodity prices are a case in point.

The final part of the report will be concerned with both the long-term and short-term aspects of creditworthiness, citing the credit-worthiness indicators on the spread sheet. If the country report is being written for the first time, historical trends on debt-servicing problems are a useful piece of information, even if difficult to obtain. There is little in the way of a history of sovereign loan problems, because these are a relatively new form of international lending. But it is interesting that a large number of Latin American countries experienced debt-servicing problems in the 1930s and countries such as Turkey have had a long history of debt crises. Australia and individual states in the United States have not been free of debt-servicing problems, a point noted in Chapter 1.

In sum, the written part of the country report should be brief and concise, concentrating on the information provided on the spread sheet. For there is no point in having a spread sheet unless the data reported on it are put to work.

Decision-Taking at Credit Committee

The decision to grant a sovereign loan will require the decision-maker to consider the issue from a very broad perspective. Chapter 3, in outlining a general framework for the supply and demand of sovereign loans, illustrated the complexities involved in this type of lending. Both the scale of commitment of funds (in relation to bank capital) and the fact that the loan is to a sovereign nation make this type of loan unique in the bank's portfolio. The country report is only a part of the information the bank needs to make an informed decision. Other considerations include:

(1)   Recognition that the spread sheet and written country report are historically based, relying on data from the past. Forecasts of key variables are not provided. However, before making a decision, the credit committee should be aware of the relevant projections. This is a difficult task, because it requires a forecast of an interdependent world economy, one of the less well developed areas of econometric forecasting.

(2)   The total exposure of sovereign lending to the country in question, not only by this bank but by other lenders.

(3)   The extent to which the riskiness of this loan is correlated with the risk associated with other types of lending. For example, a bank that is heavily exposed in loans to high technology companies in its own country should take these into consideration if considering a loan to a country also committed to the development of high technology.

Bennett (1984) used a section of his paper to provide guidelines for the construction of an efficient loan portfolio. He stressed the need to consider the entire loan portfolio of a bank:

Since concern in portfolio construction is to protect the whole bank, it makes no sense to manage pieces of portfolio in isolation from one another. Rather the foreign and domestic lending policies need to be coordinated and other bank risks (e.g. funding) should be considered simultaneously.

(Bennett, 1984, p. 159)

(4)   The interdependency of the international banking system, particularly with regard to sovereign loans. This is an important point, not only for banks considering a rescheduling agreement as an alternative to declaring a bad sovereign loan but also for banks considering an increase in their degree of sovereign loan exposure. The interdependency of the international banking system and its implications for the sovereign lender are considered in Chapter 5, reflecting the view of the author that banks involved in sovereign lending must consider the risks and rewards from a much·broader perspective than they have in the past.

5 International Financial Stability: Problems and Solutions

Since the Polish and Mexican debt-management difficulties of the early 1980s, attention has focused on the question of whether the current international debt problems will act as the catalyst for an international financial crisis and the widespread collapse of the international banking system. The purpose of this chapter is to address these issues. Some readers may take the view that these problems are not relevant to the day-to-day problems of sovereign risk analysis. It is hoped that, by this stage of the book, this group represents a very small minority. The underlying theme of the book has been to stress the need to remove sovereign risk analysis from the narrow confines it typically enjoys and to view the problems associated with it in a much broader perspective. Lenders should treat a sovereign loan as an asset in a well-diversified portfolio which, for a given risk, maximizes expected returns. Borrowers should look at this type of borrowing as a means of raising external finance, which will enhance economic development in their countries. However, both parties need to be aware of the *interdependency* of the international banking system and the unique problems created by sovereign lending within it. The purpose of this chapter is to explain this interdependency and the implications of this for the stability of the international financial system as we know it. It is hoped that, by putting the issues of sovereign lending in a global perspective, the decision-making process of both borrower and lender will be enhanced.

The chapter is organized as follows: first, a review of a number of key concepts are reviewed, including financial stability, financial crises, insolvency and illiquidity. The applicability of these terms is reviewed in the context of the international financial system. We then examine in some detail the various proposals put forward to deal with the current international financial problems.

Financial Instability, Crises, Insolvency and Illiquidity

These are terms that appear frequently in the popular press without ever being adequately defined. In economies, a system (e.g. a market for a certain good) is said to be stable when there are economic forces which ensure a return to equilibrium in the event of disequilibrium. An example of a disequilibrium in financial markets would be if the interest rate were higher than that dictated by the demand and supply of credit. The system is stable if, as a result of the implied deficient demand and/or excess supply, the interest rate declined until the disequilibrium was removed, i.e. the market cleared. The market would be unstable if there were no forces which brought this about and instead the interest rate continued on an upward spiral.

In the context of the current international debt problem, financial instability could arise if, as a result of repudiation of their debt, the LDCs provoked a run on Western banks which, in turn, was responsible for the collapse of the international financial system. It would be a situation of instability because economic forces had failed to prevent this collapse.

The terms financial 'crisis' and 'instability' have often been used interchangeably, but it is important to distinguish between the two concepts. A *crisis* describes a situation where there is a potential for recovery from the threat to the system. *Financial instability* is far more serious, because there are no economic forces which will permit the system to recover from disequilibrium.

With these concepts in mind, consider the current international situation. The Fisher–Minsky–Kindleberger description of financial crisis[1] can be used to explain the current problems. This school views the crisis as an endogenous part of the business cycle. An exogenous event is the catalyst for an upswing in the cycle, which in turn creates profitable opportunities for investment in key sectors of the economy. Prices, output and profit rates rise in these sectors and this in turn stimulates further investment. The implicit increase in the demand for finance puts an upward pressure on interest rates, assuming there is no simultaneous increase in supply. Four factors contribute to the increasing 'fragility' (Minsky, 1977) of the financial system:

(1) An increase in debt finance, especially if real interest rates are declining because the rate of inflation is rising faster than nominal rates of interest.

(2) A rising ratio of short-term debt to long-term debt.

(3) A reduction in the financial institutions' margins of safety.

(4) A general trend away from hedge finance where a unit's debt-service payments are significantly less than its receipts, to *ponzi* finance where the unit has to undertake new borrowing in order to meet existing debt-service commitments.

The term 'ponzi' finance needs further elaboration. In the literature, it is frequently asserted or implied that ponzi finance is in some way a bad thing. Indeed, the word ponzi comes from the surname of a fraudulent Boston swindler. Yet there is a distinction between firms or units which undertake to refinance their operations because this will improve the financial gearing of the unit and firms which, unless they refinance, would otherwise face the risk of bankruptcy or take-over. From the way ponzi finance is defined above, both types of unit could fit the description. For example, if debt charges are high because of high expectations of inflation (which means the rate of real amortization will be faster), refinancing current debt fits the common definition of ponzi finance but has no sinister implications. Therefore, there is a need to distinguish between 'healthy' and 'unhealthy' ponzi finance. In the description of the financial crisis below, the references apply to unhealthy forms of ponzi finance.

The increasing financial fragility exerts a further upward pressure on interest rates. A vicious circle ensues, with rising interest rates eventually provoking a refinancing crisis. At this stage the situation is one of financial crisis. But it can quickly become unstable, because these conditions will provoke 'distress selling' (Fisher, 1932) as firms that are denied refinancing opportunities are forced to liquidate their assets. These firms are unable to refinance because they are deemed to be insolvent, that is, their liabilities, excluding equity capital, exceed their net worth. However, healthy ponzi finance cases may also be affected if information problems prevent a distinction between healthy and unhealthy ponzi finance. The distress selling lowers the asset values of the firm in question. If a bank or number of banks are associated with a sufficiently large number of these insolvent firms, the banks' asset values will also decline.

This is the point at which the system may become unstable. The catalyst for the financial instability is imperfect information. If this condition holds, then the investor/depositor may react to the financial problems associated with the single firm or bank by revising down his or her estimates of the relative safety of other firms or banks (Batchelor, 1983). This reaction is known as the contagion effect: under conditions of less than perfect information, investors (depositors) perceive that the risks of insolvency (bank failure) are positively correlated across firms (banks). When the contagion effect spreads to banks and provokes bank runs, which in turn cause widespread bank failures, the financial system will collapse. Hence, the system has moved from a situation of crisis to one of instability. Intervention by the central bank acting as a lender of last resort is the usual means by which the unstable situation is averted. The lender of last resort debate is discussed in some detail in the next section (see pp. 159–63).

The real school description can be used to interpret the current sovereign debt problem as an international financial crisis, though it is not quite as straightforward as the outline given above. The debtor countries and banks highly exposed in sovereign lending were the financial units responsible for the increasing fragility of the system. But the sovereign borrowing trends of the 1970s cannot be explained by an upswing in the international business cycle. Rather, they were provoked by a number of random international shocks which were responsible for a general recession in the world economy. The effect of these random shocks on the external debt position of developing countries was described in Chapter 1 and needs no further elaboration. In addition to the demand side-effect, the shocks also had an important impact on the supply side of international credit, as members of OPEC redeposited their oil revenues in the Western banking system. The countries began to move away from hedge to unhealthy forms of ponzi external finance from the mid-1970s onwards. It was unhealthy because for most of the debtor nations which have subsequently had to reschedule, the new sovereign loans were being used to deal with fundamental disequilibria on their balance of payments, as was seen in Chapter 1. At the time, the private international banking system was praised for its intermediation in the serious current account imbalance between the OPEC nations and the non oil developing countries, which in turn was threatening a serious financial crisis. But did this intermediation permanently remove the threat of a crisis or did it only provide a temporary respite? With the benefit of hindsight, it is clear that it did the latter.

The decline in price of oil at the start of the new decade reduced the supply of international finance. However, the demand for international credit continued to rise, for a number of reasons. First, most developing countries had by this time experienced a serious reduction in their terms of trade as export volumes and prices dropped in response to world recession, which in turn had been provoked by the two oil price rises in the 1970s. Secondly, almost simultaneously with the decline in oil revenues going to the member nations of OPEC, there was a swing to tight money policy in most Western economies. As a consequence, world interest rates began to rise. This contributed to serious debt-servicing problems for highly geared LDCs, which with rising current account deficits pushed the developing nations into an unhealthy ponzi finance situation with respect to their external debt positions.

The other three characteristics of financial fragility were also present. The Euroloan markets encouraged the development of short-term to medium-term lending rather than long-term lending. Debt finance as a proportion of total external finance rose dramatically from the early 1970s. We can also question whether the lenders' margins of safety on their sovereign loans were adequate, given the common belief among bankers that this type of lending was safe because countries could not go bankrupt.

These events were responsible for an increasing degree of international financial fragility. Mexico's announcement of a moratorium on external debt payments in August 1982 provoked a crisis on internatonal financial markets. Like the purely domestic situation described above, a key feature of the crisis has been the large number of refinancing agreements, which became necessary as debtor nations could no longer meet their debt-servicing obligations. But it is worth stressing that, unlike the domestic scene where individual firms were the precarious financial units, it is the debtor countries and international banks highly exposed in sovereign lending that threaten the stability of the financial system. To date, this instability (which would have as its main feature the collapse of the international financial system) has been averted through the successful rescheduling of sovereign loan obligations. But, before the details of these packages are discussed, it is helpful to clarify the difference between insolvency and illiquidity as these terms are applied to the international system.

The reader has already been provided with the formal definition of the *insolvent* firm: it is any firm with a negative net worth. In the Western economies a court of law declares a firm insolvent and there are usually well-defined bankruptcy procedures by which some of the creditors recover part of their investment. A firm is said to be *illiquid* when it has a positive net worth but lacks the means to meet its maturing liabilities when they come due and are payable.

Turning to the current international situation, these terms must be applied at two levels. First, there are the problem debtor nations. It is difficult if not impossible to declare a country insolvent, because to do so implies the belief that the country has a negative net worth. But is this term applicable to developing countries which seek external finance in order to generate higher income streams in the future? Put another way, it would be difficult to attach a value to a country's total assets, given that future economic growth rates will be crucial to determining what these values are. We would have to define a time period for debt-servicing beyond which a country's net worth is declared negative. Secondly, there would also be legal difficulties: the current international legal system gives no court of law the power to declare a country bankrupt. Finally, even if a country could be declared legally bankrupt, what action could be taken in the interest of external investors? The sale of a nation's assets is not a feasible solution. These factors have added to the problems of lenders who are trying to assess the riskiness of the loan. Until recently, bank lending behaviour suggested that a sovereign loan was riskless precisely because a country could not be declared bankrupt. But as these nations became increasingly illiquid, unable to service their debt beyond a few months and in some cases a few weeks, bank perceptions of riskiness rose. However, it is probably fair to argue that lenders have not yet defined an appropriate risk class for sovereign loans. These ambiguities mean one must be wary of statements of the sort made by Professor Cline:

> The most fundamental policy issue today concerning international debt is whether the major debtor countries are illiquid or insolvent.
>
> (Cline, 1984, p. 39)

It would be a pity to see policy-makers concentrating on an issue that is difficult if not impossible to resolve.

In addition, the terms insolvency and illiquidity need to be applied at the international bank level. Loans made by banks appear on the asset side of their balance sheet, but a bad loan implies a reduction in assets. A bank is said to face a liquidity problem if it lacks the means to meet its maturing liabilities. It is worth noting that for a bank, the 'maturing' of liabilities can occur very suddenly if there is a run on the bank by depositors. A bank with a negative net worth is insolvent. Like any firm that performs badly, a sufficient number of bad loans can cause the nominal value of bank shares to decline, lowering the value of total share capital. For example, investors in American banks have reacted negatively to the high sovereign loan exposure of these banks. A recent study by Sachs and Kyle (1985) finds evidence (based on a sample of 62 US commercial banks) that bank exposure to Latin American country debt did depress bank stock market prices after August 1982. The question is whether a bank that is highly exposed in sovereign lending can ever be declared insolvent because of this type of exposure. We can give an affirmative answer if asset values of the banks decline by a sufficient amount. However, for highly exposed banks in sovereign lending, the answer is not as unambiguous as it first appears, because of the conceptual and practical problems associated with the declaration of a bad sovereign loan identified earlier (see p. 149).

It is the imprecise nature of the term insolvency as applied to the sovereign loan that is at the heart of the current international financial problems. If countries were declared bankrupt, then individuals would identify the problem banks and react accordingly. This, of course, could be the cause of financial instability, because of the contagion effect. However, this seems an unlikely source of instability, given the near impossibility of declaring a nation bankrupt. But the ambiguity surrounding the nation's financial position could itself be the cause of instability, because of the uncertainty it creates. Recall that during a crisis it is imperfect information that initiates bank runs and the subsequent collapse of the financial system. The threat to stability exists because the crisis described earlier has not yet been resolved. The question we must address next is: are there solutions to the current crisis that could prevent the international financial system from becoming unstable? Several proposals have been made, some attracting considerable attention in the financial press. These are considered in the next section.

Proposals for International Financial Stability

The Non-Interventionist Option

Many policy-makers and bankers are of the opinion that new forms of official international action to deal with the problems of debtor countries and highly exposed banks are unnecessary. In support of their case, they cite recent developments such as the success of the rescheduling packages and regulations on international lending adopted by the US authorities. It is argued that debt-servicing difficulties can be solved on a case-by-case basis, with the IMF acting as an intermediary between the private Western banks and the borrowing countries, while new regulations will discourage future excessive exposure in this type of debt. However, these measures give all parties a false sense of security and only partially address the problems at the heart of the crisis. This becomes evident if we scrutinize the contents of the rescheduling packages, the new forms of sovereign lending that emerged in the early 1980s, and the details of new US regulations on international lending.

CONTENTS OF THE RESCHEDULING PACKAGES

Cline (1984, p. 31) and *The Bank of England Quarterly Bulletin* (March 1984, table on p. 55) summarize the main characteristics of recent commercial loan rescue operations.[2] These include:

(1)   *The Use of Official Bridging Loans:* These are loans granted by the Bank for International Settlements (BIS), the US Treasury and the US Federal Reserve. The purpose of the loans is to bridge the gap between the time when the borrowing country declares its inability to

service its debt under the current arangement and the time when the IMF and private banks can assemble an acceptable loan package. As such, they are short-term loans and typically have to be repaid within 90 days. During 1983, Brazil tried unsuccessfully to extend the maturity of its BIS loan.

(2) *External Debt Rescheduling:* This is the central feature of the packages. Until Mexico's declaration of a moratorium on debt payments in 1982, the IMF had provided member countries with temporary financial resources if these countries were experiencing problems of illiquidity not deemed by the IMF to be the result of a 'fundamental disequilibrium' on the country's balance of payments. But the IMF provisions had been developed for a pegged exchange rate world, where international capital was largely immobile. By 1982, the IMF had come to realize that its stand-by facilities would not be an effective means of dealing with the international debt problem. For there was a third party involved: the private international banks. If the IMF had intervened unilaterally to bail out these countries, the incentive effect on private lenders (not to mention borrowers!) could have exacerbated the problems in the future. In any case, this was not a viable course of action, given the magnitude of the debt problem in relation to the IMF reserves.

The obvious short-term solution was to insist that IMF funding would only be forthcoming if the private banks agreed to reschedule their part of the loans. In this way there were no free-riders, that is, banks which improved the quality of their loan portfolio through the IMF intervention without assuming any additional risk themselves.

The main component of the packages has been the rescheduling of between 60 per cent and 100 per cent of medium-term and long-term (and in some cases short-term) debt falling due to the commercial banks over a period of between 12 and 24 months. Non-sovereign private debt has been largely excluded from the negotiations. The average package includes an agreement to repay this rescheduled principal over a period of 7 to 8 years, including a grace period of between 2.5 and 4 years. The packages have also included fees, ranging from 0.5 per cent to 1.5 per cent depending on the country and the position of the bank in the negotiating team, i.e. whether the bank is an agent, a lead manager, a co-manager or a participant. The spreads on the new loan agreements are high if compared with the original agreement. For example, Mexico's 1983 package includes a spread over LIBOR of 2 per cent compared with an average spread of 0·9 per cent over LIBOR for new loans negotiated between 1978 and 1980.

(3)   *IMF Programme:* An IMF economic adjustment programme in exchange for the use of IMF credit facilities is an integral part of the packages. Private banks have insisted that an agreed programme of recovery be in place before new loans are granted. Clearly, bankers are confident that with IMF intervention of this sort, debt problems will be alleviated. The adjustment programmes normally involve the government's agreeing to tight controls over money supply growth rates, budget deficits and inflation, an end to government intervention in the price system in the form of food subsidies, wage indexation, etc., a ceiling on nominal wage rises, a reduction in trade barriers, and devaluation. It is too early to say whether these measures will restore the health of these economies.

(4)   *Interbank and Trade Facility Provisions:* The packages usually include some provision for the continuation of trade facilities and deal with the problem of keeping the interbank network open for foreign branches of debtor country banks.

(5)   *New Money:* The rescue packages have required borrowers to meet all their current interest obligations. This is important to the cosmetics of the packages, because a failure to meet interest obligations may force the banks into technical declarations of default. In order to facilitate the repayment of interest, creditor banks have contributed 'new money', a certain percentage of their existing exposure.

The features of the rescheduling packages illustrate that these packages are really new loan agreements undertaken by sovereign borrower and lender, with the IMF overseeing the conditions of the agreement. They have made the declaration of bad sovereign loans unnecessary, an event which would have serious implications for the balance sheets of the highly exposed banks. However, the agreements will only succeed in averting a collapse of the international financial system if new loans are the optimal means of dealing with the underlying problem. But are they? Recall from the earlier chapters the shocks to the world economy, which were largely responsible for creating the severe balance of payments problems faced by many countries during the 1970s. These included the oil price rises and, toward the end of the 1970s, the rapid rise in real interest rates. Widespread world recession further exacerbated Third World balance of payments difficulties. These problems in turn created an incentive for these countries to seek relief on the international capital markets via sovereign borrowings. If random shocks are again responsible for world recession in the late 1980s, when these rescheduled sovereign loans come due, the international financial system could well be faced with another debt crisis. Provided the entire banking system is prepared to reschedule *ad infinitum*, the current method of dealing with the problem will prevent a financial collapse. This really involves acceptance by both the banks and their shareholders of the idea that there is no such thing as a bad sovereign loan. However, the lack of *formality* associated with the current system of rescheduling makes this unlikely.

NEW FORMS OF SOVEREIGN LENDING: NIFS AND FRNS

In addition to the well-publicized rescheduling of developing country sovereign external debt, the emergence of Note Issuance Facilities (NIFs) has given rise to a new form of sovereign lending. Using the definition employed by the *Bank of England Quarterly Bulletin* (March 1985, p. 39), Note Issuance Facilities is a generic term, which includes revolving underwriting facilities (RUFs), note purchase facilities (NPFs) and Euronote facilities. All are a type of commercial paper. To quote an excellent description of NIFs published in the *Financial Times*:

> ... banks underwrite the continuous sale by their clients of short term securities or euronotes to investors, thereby providing a guarantee to the borrower that funds will be available over the medium term. (*Financial Times*, 9 May 1985, p. 20)

To the extent that the holders of these notes are the original or some other purchasing bank and the borrowing party is a government, these facilities will constitute actual or committed sovereign debt.

The participants in this market are attracted to NIFs for different reasons. NIFs permit all parties to avoid a commitment to medium-term fixed rates. The borrower has more flexibility because, unlike the conventional Eurocredit, the credit line need not be drawn down at specified dates but can be drawn up and down according to the needs of the borrower.

NIFs permit banks to arrange a medium-term credit line by using short-term debt. In addition, because these facilities are off balance sheet, the capital adequacy requirements are less stringent. Investors are attracted to this type of commercial paper because the short maturity of the three- to six-month notes minimises the capital, interest and exchange rate risk associated with floating rate notes and medium-term certificates of deposit.

However, a directive issued by the Bank of England in April 1985 may make NIFs less attractive. For the purposes of assessing capital adequacy, NIFs are to be treated as contingent liabilities and will carry a weighting of 0·5 in the computation of a bank's risk asset ratio, whether or not the facility has been drawn. By way of contrast, drawn loans to other banks carry a weight of 0·2. This intervention reflects concern by the Bank of England that these facilities have the potential of becoming a form of intermediation if the underwriting banks are left holding the paper or other banks are the investors. Demonstrating the same concern, the Japanese authorities are to introduce a weighting of 0·3 for all undrawn facilities in April 1986 and US regulators are expected to introduce a comprehensive set of ratios by the end of 1985.

The relevance of these new facilities to the sovereign risk problem arises when the purchasers of the commercial paper are banks and the borrower is a government. Recent figures published by the *Bank of England Quarterly Review* (March, 1985, p. 39) indicate that the market has grown from just under $0·25 billion in 1981 to just under $5 billion in 1984. Throughout this period, more than half the borrowers were from OECD countries and, in 1983 and 1984, this group made up 93 per cent and 88 per cent of the total, respectively. In 1981, 52 per cent of the total were sovereign borrowers, but this figure fell to 26 per cent in 1984. Other borrowers are either industrial or financial entities. Non-OECD borrowers have included Singapore, South Korea, India, Oman and Saudi Arabia. The *Bank of England Quarterly Review* (June 1985) estimates that only 20 per cent of completed NIFs have actually been drawn.

These figures suggest that the number of sovereign borrowers participating in this market is relatively small: they tend to be governments with a very high credit rating. There are no figures for the percentage of the notes purchased by banks, but it is generally believed that less than 10 per cent of the notes have had to be taken into the books of the underwriting bank(s). None the less, the recent action taken by the central bank authorities reflects their concern about the possibility that NIFs could undermine the capital adequacy of participating banks.

From the standpoint of sovereign risk, this type of commercial paper has the potential of increasing a bank's sovereign exposure in a less direct way than was true of the type of sovereign lending typical of the 1970s. If international banks had enough of this type of sovereign commercial paper on their books, the implications for the stability of the banking system would be the same should the sovereign borrower encounter debt repayment difficulties. However, it is too early to form an opinion because, to date, the size of this market has been relatively small, the proportion of sovereign borrowers is low, and the number of banks holding this commercial paper as a percentage of total investors is unknown.

Floating Rate Notes (FRNs) have existed since 1970, but did not show a rapid growth rate until the beginning of the 1980s. Marketability is the main attraction of FRNs and they have been issued by commercial banks, private corporations and governments. Since 1982, only creditworthy developing country governments have had access to these markets, although Brazil and Mexico issued FRNs prior to their recent debt-servicing problems. According to the World Bank (1985, p. 122), commercial banks have purchased approximately 70 per cent of all FRNs. When the FRN has been issued by a government, this will represent a form of sovereign debt. But, like NIFs, it is too early to judge the extent to which this type of security could threaten the stability of the international financial system.

US REGULATIONS ON INTERNATIONAL LENDING

The US regulatory agencies – the Federal Deposit Insurance Corporation, the Federal Reserve Board and the Office of the Comptroller of the Currency – have jointly issued new regulations on foreign lending by US banks. The new rules were announced by the Federal Reserve in 1984[3] to comply with the International Lending Supervision Act passed by Congress in 1983.

The first of the new rules requires banks to use current income to maintain a special reserve (an allocated transfer risk reserve or ATRR) against risks arising from international loans or other assets. An annual review by the regulatory authorities will establish which international assets are risky enough to require an ATRR, the size of the ATRR and, if an ATRR is already in place, whether it can be reduced. In the first year, the ATRR will be 10 per cent of the principal amount of the asset, rising to 15 per cent in subsequent years. Instead of establishing an ATRR, a bank may write down the asset, but it must then replenish its allowance for possible loan losses. To determine whether an ATRR is necessary, two questions are raised:

(1)   Has the quality of an international loan been lowered because borrowers have, over a long period of time, been unable to meet their repayment schedules?

(2)   Are the prospects for restoring orderly debt-service close to nil?

Other rules relate to the reporting procedure for country exposures and the treatment of front-end fees. In the case of the former, the required frequency of reporting country exposures by US banks has been increased, and the Country Exposure Report Form (introduced in 1977) modified. Front-end fees must be deferred and amortized over the life of the loan rather than treated as income in the year in which they are charged, a practice which encouraged international lending in order to raise earnings. The only exception to this rule will be those fees identified as a reimbursement of direct costs.

The new regulations are the most comprehensive of all those introduced by the central banks of the major lending countries. The close scrutiny by US regulators will give rise to more careful consideration of any new sovereign lending by banks and, therefore, sovereign loan exposure should decline. However, the regulations only apply to American banks and, more important, do nothing for the problems created by increased sovereign loan exposures up to February 1984. For these reasons, they cannot be regarded as a comprehensive solution to the sovereign debt problem.

The Case for Intervention: Proposals for International Agencies

Several suggestions appear under this heading. They have been put forward as potential solutions to the current international financial problems and range from a proposal for an international lender of last resort to call for a new role for the IMF. To understand the current debate, it is helpful to review the long-running dispute over the role of a central bank. The arguments are best illustrated by looking at two schools of thought: the banking school and the currency school.

The passage of the Bank of England Act in 1844 was a victory for the proponents of the currency school.[4] This group believed the primary function of the central bank should be the stabilization of prices through strict adherence to the quantity theory of money. This reflected the earlier acceptance of the Palmer Rule in 1832, which had called for a fixed volume of securities and a passive exchange of gold against notes. Strict control over the money supply took place until 1914: over this period the average annual rate of growth of the money stock was less than 1 per cent compared with a 2·5 per cent average annual rate of growth of output.[5] The currency school was of the opinion that strict money supply growth rules would eliminate speculative manias because speculators would come to realize that there was no accommodating institution for their activities. This in turn would eliminate monetary crises, since (the school argued) these were caused by speculative manias. However, the school was proved wrong by the crises of 1847, 1857 and 1866, when the government was forced to suspend the Act as reserves held at the Bank of England dwindled to nothing.

Although the banking school had been defeated in 1844, it did not disappear from the scene. The 1914 Bank of England Act adopted some of its ideas. This group argued that the role of the central bank should revolve around the prevention of financial crises rather than strict control over money supply growth rates. The school called for a measure which would guarantee the quality of issue through strict convertibility to gold. In the 1914 Act, the strict money supply growth rule was replaced by a discretionary monetary policy, a concession to the banking school. The Bank of England would continue to control growth rates in the money supply, but not at the expense of financial crises. Over time, the Bank has assumed responsibility for the preservation of financial stability in the banking system, although in an informal way. The deposit of reserves at the Bank by private banks is a convention rather than a rule and, although the Bank has no specific lender of last resort function in the British banking system, it has de facto acted in this capacity. This was illustrated in recent times by its role in the secondary banking crisis in the UK in 1973–5 and in the nationalization of Johnson Matthey Bankers in 1984.

The central bank function of the Federal Reserve in the USA has evolved in much the same way as in the UK although there has always been a greater formal stress on the preservation of financial stability. In particular, the Glass Steagall Banking Act passed in 1934 gave the Federal Reserve the authority to adjust its reserve requirements. Prior to this Act, the reserve requirement could only be altered through legislation. The 1934 Act also called for the establishment of a deposit insurance scheme, a measure designed to increase public confidence in the US banking system. The recent intervention by the Reserve in the Continental Illinois case suggests that it continues to see the preservation of a stable financial system as one of its primary duties.

This brief historical background will go some way in helping the reader to understand the present debate on whether the current international problems could best be dealt with through the establishment of an International Lender of Last Resort (ILLR). Below, the arguments for and against such a body will be discussed. Following this, I shall address the question of whether an ILLR is the optimal solution to the international crisis. Finally, I shall turn to an alternative, an International Financial Coordination Agency, of which the main objective is the preservation of financial stability at the international level. However, and this is the important point, the means by which it would achieve this stability are very different from that suggested by the historical evolution of the domestic central bank. This is mainly because of the unique features of the sovereign loan market.

AN INTERNATIONAL LENDER OF LAST RESORT

Several recent publications have debated the case for and against an international lender of last resort. Two worthy of note are the papers by Guttenhag and Herring (1983) and by Beenstock (1986). Guttenhag and Herring argue in favour of an ILLR while Beenstock is against any LLR, be it domestic or international. Let us begin with a review of the Beenstock arguments against a lender of last resort. As the reader will come to realize, these arguments are consistent with the currency school interpretation of a central bank, although they have been put more succinctly and in terms of the financial problems faced by the modern world economy. The Beenstock thesis accepts the idea that imperfect information is the key to explaining why runs on the banking system occur, but he argues that, if rational economic agents had full information on the financial position of banks, the bank runs would be confined to insolvent banks. Banks experiencing problems of illiquidity do not need a LLR because in efficient capital markets new equity capital will be forthcoming. Insolvent banks should be allowed to go under. Full information would prevent the contagion effect from causing a run on one bank spreading to the entire system. Professor Beenstock argues that banks are like any other business and, therefore, should not have access to a lender of last resort if they get into financial trouble. The stability of the financial system will not be undermined by individual bank failures, because full disclosure of information will assure the public about the financial viability of remaining banks.

The Beenstock argument suffers from a number of problems. First, banks are different from other firms and this difference explains why banks are more likely to face the problem of runs on them. To see why, consider the functions which a bank performs. As Santomero (1984) has pointed out, the reasons for the existence of a bank fall into roughly two categories. First, banks offer their customers an asset transformation service, in the form of the diversification of risky assets and the evaluation of these assets prior to purchase. This, of course, will include the granting of loans to creditworthy borrowers. Secondly, the bank acts as a financial intermediary in any economy where money is the medium of exchange. This dual role means banks are like a multiproduct firm. Also, the banks have joint production functions: they rely on depositors, who employ their cash-management services in order to 'produce' other financial services, the most obvious being their lending facilities. Although joint production is not in any way unique to banks, the dependence on deposits as a key factor input in the production process is. No other firm exists where the supplier of a crucial factor input is also a customer demanding one of the bank's products. This interdependency between customer utility functions and bank production functions reduces the flexibility of the bank when it comes to responding to dissatisfaction on the part of its customers. In the typical firm, action can be initiated if the firm finds a large number of faulty products being returned. If the problem is rectified, the firm's financial position should not be undermined. Now consider the withdrawal of deposits by dissatisfied customers, concerned with the viability of their bank. Immediately, the ability of the bank to continue to produce its output is undermined. There is no lag of the sort enjoyed by the non banking firm, because the supplier of the bank's factor input and the demander of its product are the same individual. The implied inflexibility in turn makes it difficult for a bank to recover from a run without some provision of resources that will enable it to keep producing.

Secondly, it is important to recognize that it is rational for depositors to withdraw their deposits from illiquid banks, not just insolvent banks. To understand this it is necessary to review the reasons for holding a bank deposit. Non or low interest earning deposits are normally held in exchange for the money transmission services banks have on offer. Banks also offer high interest earning deposit accounts, the capital value of which will probably rise over time. In this sense the latter type of deposit represents an investment and may be treated as an imperfect substitute for other forms of investment, such as the purchase of equity holdings in a firm. However, the first type of deposit (a 'money transmission' deposit) is in no sense a substitute for any type of investment even though, in law, the depositor is a creditor. The owner of the deposit is incurring a 100 per cent downside risk: with the capital value of this type of deposit largely unchanged over time, then if depositors begin to withdraw their deposits, remaining depositors only stand to lose. This is because the *liquidity* offered by the bank is a critical part of its money transmission service and a significant withdrawal of deposits will impair the ability of the bank to offer this service. Hence, the depositor has nothing to gain if the bank fails and everything to lose if it does. This is quite different from the case of an equity holding in a firm or even a high interest earning bank deposit. In these cases, there is an incentive to hold on to the investment if, for example, there is a sudden sale of shares by a large number of investors. This is because there is a chance that the shareholder will profit from a subsequent increase in the share values. A similar 'upside' risk can be observed in the case of the high interest bearing deposit. But given the 100 per cent downside risk associated with a money transmission deposit, the depositor is rational to withdraw his/her funds at the first hint of liquidity problems, because such problems will undermine the bank's ability to offer this liquidity service. Therefore, illiquid banks may well be subject to bank runs.

What of runs on the *entire* banking system? Proponents of the Beenstock thesis would likely respond to the above criticism by claiming that, if full disclosure of information were required, depositors and investors alike would be able to distinguish between insolvent and illiquid banks. This in turn would rule out runs on banks with liquidity problems, because no rational depositor would think it prudent to withdraw deposits. Insolvent banks would be subject to bank runs, but these should be allowed to fail in any case. As was pointed out in the preceding paragraph, even illiquid banks may be subject to runs. However, let us pursue the argument that full disclosure will eliminate contagion effects and therefore prevent a run on the banking system. First, we have to question the meaning of full disclosure. Beenstock makes the following comment on what is meant by full disclosure:

> Banks should disclose information on their lending by sector, country and maturity as well as providing details of bad debts and charge-offs in terms of these categories. (Beenstock, 1984, p. 23)

At several points in the paper, Beenstock suggests that full disclosure as defined above would bring British banks into line with the disclosure requirements of non-financial institutions, which are covered by the 1948 Companies Act. The 1967 Act did go some way to achieve this objective. Banks were required to publish the full details of their profits and any hidden reserves. However, neither Act requires businesses to disclose the *composition* of their receivables and payables. To do so could breach confidentiality and seriously weaken the firm's competitiveness and bargaining position with respect to its customers. In turn this would reduce the volume of business activity undertaken and profitability. Yet to know the composition of the bank's assets, bad loans, etc., would be critical to the successful elimination of the contagion effect in the banking system.

Another problem with the full disclosure argument relates to the implicit assumption that a 'bad' loan can always be identified. The Beenstock case rests on this being possible. This assumption is very important when it comes to the distinction between the insolvent bank and one with liquidity problems. The near impossibility of declaring a country insolvent was noted earlier (see p. 149). Given these difficulties, how will it ever be possible to designate as insolvent banks that are highly exposed in sovereign lending unless a country actually repudiates its debt? In this sense, sovereign lending represents a unique type of lending for a bank. No doubt there are other types of domestic bank lending for which the term 'bad' loan is misleading. Cooper (1984), in a very good account of the 'lifeboat' solution to the UK secondary banking crisis from 1973 to 1975, comments:

> It follows that any action . . . to solve the liquidity problems of individual borrowing institutions, taken for the public good, cannot in practice be totally disentangled from the solvency problems and potential solvency problems of such institutions: any such mechanism will thus inevitably involve somebody – Bank of England, clearing banker or any other participant – in undertaking credit risks beyond what they would normally regard as prudent limits. (Cooper, 1984, p. 14)

This quote demonstrates the difficulties of distinguishing between insolvency and illiquidity in a domestic crisis. At the international level, the problems are far more complex.

To summarize the salient points made above, banks are different from other firms in that a large part of the production of their services depends on deposits. Bank 'money transmission' deposits differ from equity investments because the depositor incurs a risk that is almost 100 per cent downside. The contagion effect in the banking system will not be ruled out under full disclosure unless all bad debt can be clearly defined and banks are required to disclose the detailed composition of their assets and liabilities. The latter condition would undermine the profitability of bank activity to the extent that the services provided by them would be curtailed. All businesses, including banks, profit from taking risks, but the scale of risk-taking would be seriously impaired if full disclosure of the type necessary to prevent bank runs was the requirement.

The Beenstock case against a lender of last resort rests on the assumption that these very strict conditions can be met. As Beenstock himself notes, if there is a possibility of a run on the entire banking system a LLR is necessary because this type of risk is uninsurable. It is not feasible to expect capitalist economies to meet the strict conditions required to rule out the possibility of bank runs because their imposition would undermine what is at the heart of the capitalist system, the ability of a firm (be it a bank or any other business) to profit by taking risks.

Beenstock's thesis concentrated on the domestic LLR, but his ideas are easily carried over to make a case against an International LLR. Having pointed out the pitfalls of the argument against the LLR, a strong case can be made in favour of domestic LLRs. It is now time to address the question of whether it is necessary and/or feasible to establish an international central bank with LLR responsibilities, keeping in mind that we are considering methods by which financial instability can be averted.

Guttenhag and Herring (1983) are somewhat ambiguous in their presentation of the case for an ILLR. To the extent that they do commit themselves, they appear to favour the establishment of an ILLR in line with proposals for a domestic LLR made by Thornton and Bagehot in 1802 and 1873, respectively. These classical contributions stressed the need for a LLR with well-defined responsibilities to the financial system. To avert financial crises, the LLR would lend to all solvent banks that were experiencing liquidity problems. However, there are several difficulties with the case for a 'classical' ILLR. First, the distinction between an insolvent and illiquid international bank becomes ambiguous when the bank is highly exposed in sovereign lending, a point which was made earlier. Secondly, the traditional form of LLR intervention has entailed an increase in the money supply to support the illiquid banks threatened by bank runs. Hence, if the classical idea were applied at the international level, national governments would no longer independently control their money supplies. In addition, if the ILLR was going to stand any chance of success when it came to distinguishing between solvent and insolvent banks, it would require information on the operations of banks within national banking systems. Again, this would encroach upon the monopoly enjoyed by governments in the regulation of their banking systems. Finally, the ILLR would encounter the usual problems of moral hazard. This issue is considered in more detail below. Suffice it to say that, although the moral hazard problems would not rule out an ILLR, the infringements on national sovereignty and the 'bad' loan problem could well make it an unfeasible proposition.

We must also question whether a 'classical' ILLR is the appropriate solution, given the underlying causes of the international financial crisis. The ILLR would solve the liquidity problems of international banks and therefore minimize the probability of a collapse of the international financial system. However, this solution concentrates solely on the *supply side* of international lending problems. It would do nothing for the demand side, that is, the difficulties arising from severe balance of payments problems in developing countries. These countries temporarily averted the problems inherent in fundamental disequilibria by borrowing heavily on the private international capital markets. An ILLR would leave the demand side of the problem largely unchecked, only playing an indirect role through any restrictions it placed on forms of international lending.

AN INTERNATIONAL FINANCIAL CO-ORDINATION AGENCY

At this point, the reader may be inclined to conclude that, although the Beenstock argument against a LLR may be invalid, the conditions required for a successful ILLR are not likely to be satisfied. However, this does not rule out the need for an international agency with some of the functions normally associated with a central bank. The central objective of this International Financial Co-ordination Agency (IFCA) would be the preservation of international financial stability. The means by which it achieved its goal would differ from the standard functions we normally associate with a domestic central bank, such as control over the money supply, a LLR function, and the placement of government debt on the most favourable terms possible. However, the international financial system is unique and as such the solution to its stability problems is also unique.

As was observed earlier in this chapter, the main cause of financial fragility has been a number of random shocks to the supply and demand sides of private sovereign lending. Since it is this problem which lies at the heart of the crisis, the IFCA would intervene to minimize the effects of the shocks. In particular, the IMF's role in the negotiation of the rescheduling packages would be *formalized* and given to the IFCA. The rescheduling has postponed the repayment of borrower external debt and, provided there are no future random shocks of the type experienced in the 1970s, debt-servicing difficulties should not arise. But it would be naive in the extreme to rule out the possibility of future random shocks. In the absence of a formalized procedure designed specifically to deal with the debt-servicing problems of sovereign debt caused by random shocks to the world economy, the next round of sovereign debtor problems could prove too great a strain for the international banking system. Instead of a mere financial crisis, a general loss of confidence could provoke widespread collapse of the Western banking system. The likelihood of this occurring rises with every round of tension associated with a major debtor country experiencing renewed debt-servicing problems. *Formalization* of the rescheduling process would force lender and borrower alike to recognize the *long-term* nature of the sovereign debt problem.

It is important to stress that the IFCA would not assume the debt burden itself, currently estimated to amount to more than $800 billion for developing countries alone. This would be neither possible nor desirable. Related to this, it is worth noting that several schemes have been put forward, all of which share in common the transfer of lender responsibility from the private banking system to a public body. The real problem with these schemes is the capital resources they demand. The public body would require a large capital injection if it was to assume the debt, a point noted by Cline (1984, p. 134). Suppose the total amount of debt assumed was $800 billion. Under full capital backing, $40 billion would have to be raised if 10 per cent of the capital was paid in with a contingent liability of $400 billion. It is doubtful whether Western governments would agree to raise this sum, especially when they observe the apparent success of the rescheduling procedure in dealing with the problem. Apart from funding difficulties, the 'bail out' would have an adverse effect on borrower and lender incentives, and thus could well increase the risks associated with international lending. This 'moral hazard' problem requires further consideration.

Moral hazard is a term borrowed from the insurance literature. If a contract of insurance is agreed upon by two parties, then the agreement shifts the risks of the event being insured. The existence of the insurance alters the incentive structure for the insured party and quite possibly may alter his/her behaviour. For example, if a household takes out comprehensive insurance on the contents of the house, the existence of the insurance policy may make the occupants less careful when it comes to protection of the house from intruders. This is a classic moral hazard problem and is obviously costly to the insurer. Costs are minimized by offering deductible insurance.

If a public agency were to bail out a bank by assuming responsibility for sovereign debt, the risk profile for lenders would be dramatically altered and, as a consequence, the international lending process could involve undertakings of risk which would be greater than they are now. The only way of preventing this would be new measures to control sovereign lending.

An International Financial Co-ordination Agency which assumed the responsibilities outlined above would also create moral hazard problems on the borrowing and lending sides. Although this is a problem in both domestic and international banking, sovereign borrower moral hazard creates unique problems for international finance. These are considered after the problems of lender moral hazard have been reviewed.

Moral hazard on the lending side arises whenever the banking system has a lender of last resort. The LLR alters the risk profile of the loan and may cause banks to agree to riskier loan proposals because of the protection provided by the LLR. A further problem occurs when a bank in trouble attempts to conceal the information from a LLR in the hope that it can ride out the storm without LLR intervention. However, these difficulties are nothing new to the banking scene and typically have been dealt with through the LLR's power to make the final judgement on whether a bank is illiquid or insolvent.

As was noted above, the implications of an ILLR are such that it does not seem a feasible solution to the current difficulties. Hence, the IFCA would not assume a direct LLR role on the lending side. This task would remain with domestic central banks, which would undertake to minimize lender moral hazard. However, the IFCA would exert pressure on domestic central banks to eliminate the current gaps that exist in the assumption of responsibility for some international banks. Guttenhag and Herring (1983, pp. 20–1) identify three types of international banks that do not receive adequate coverage under the current arrangements:

(1)   Banks with their headquarters in countries with no LLR facility, for example, Luxemburg.

(2)   Banks with their headquarters in countries with inconvertible currencies and/or foreign exchange shortages.

(3)   Subsidiary banks with uncertain access to LLR facilities.

The newly created IFCA would work to get member countries to agree to fill these gaps. Once an agreement was reached, the IFCA would act on behalf of all member countries to ensure that an adequate level of reserves was being held by each domestic central bank to meet its obligations. In the case where joint action of domestic central banks was required, the IFCA could adjudicate if the practical difficulties of distinguishing between illiquidity and insolvency created friction between the member banks.

On the borrowing side, the IFCA would have a more direct role because the sovereign borrowing creates unique moral hazard problems. When a bank makes a domestic loan to a private firm, collateral is demanded to discourage default by the borrower. To prevent the careless application of the funds, the bank may threaten the borrower with explicit penalties. Or it may place credit ceilings on customers. In the case of moral hazard with respect to the sovereign borrower, similar remedies are not available. Again, this is because there is no recourse open to the lender in the event of outright repudiation by a sovereign borrower. The bank cannot demand collateral and, if it imposes penalties in the form of credit restrictions, it could well provoke default, an event which is not in the lender's interest.

The IFCA could be quite effective in minimizing moral hazard problems among sovereign borrowers. It would begin by persuading borrowing countries that it is in their interest to convince the lending banks that the probability of outright repudiation is close to zero. This would lower the cost of borrowing and, ultimately, the cost of economic development. Member nations of the IFCA (borrower and lender alike) would also grant this body the discretionary power to intervene in a member's economy, should the nation encounter economic difficulties that undermined its ability to meet its debt-servicing obligations. Formal authority of this nature would discourage carelessness in the use of sovereign loans. IMF adjustment programmes, a feature of the rescheduling packages, are similar to what is being proposed here. However, they have caused a high degree of resentment on the part of the troubled debtor nations, because at the time the original loan was negotiated there was no agreement that the IMF would intervene in the event of debt-servicing difficulties. The debtor countries have resisted the adjustment programmes proposed by the IMF largely because of their informal nature. In addition, economists continue to debate the issue of whether or not the adjustment programmes will achieve their objective. The IMF (see *World Economic Outlook*, 1983, pp. 137–40) has found some evidence to support the idea that such measures have been effective in maintaining and/or restoring economic order, though the evidence is weak and it is too early to judge their effects on economic growth.

However, there is no doubting that the role of the IMF has had a significant positive impact on lender confidence, which in turn has defused the crisis. The new IFCA could continue this function, but with the explicit objective of minimizing moral hazard among sovereign borrowers. This would lower the cost of sovereign borrowing and maintain lender confidence with respect to this type of lending. Borrowing nations must realize that, if external finance is used as a means of speeding up economic development, economic independence is reduced. If the finance comes in the form of foreign direct investment, independence is lost in part of the production process. If it is in the form of sovereign borrowing, independence will be sacrificed if the country encounters difficulties in servicing its debt. It is for the developing country's government to decide whether this external capital dependence is optimal for the country and this in turn will depend on its social welfare function. But once the decision to import capital is made, the country must play the game. It is worth noting that this argument can be extended to those industrialized nations (for example, the USA) which have chosen to finance their deficits through external borrowing.

The recent rescheduling negotiations have pointed to another difficulty the IFCA would encounter. This is the incentive to 'free ride' on the part of the 'marginal' international banks: those banks with a small exposure in sovereign loans. Banks in this category would gain from an IFCA, assuming that the latter is successful in minimizing international financial instability. But, unlike banks highly exposed in sovereign lending, the success of the IFCA would not be undermined if marginal banks opt out of membership. Hence, by not joining, marginal banks would free ride: they would derive an external benefit from the IFCA without having to pay the costs of membership. To avoid this problem, banks from non-member nations would have to be excluded from international banking activities involving sovereign lending. This could create a black market in this form of lending, because some borrowing nations would also opt to avoid IFCA monitoring. However, the size of this market would be small, because no bank highly exposed in this form of lending would have an incentive to free ride.

As has been noted, the primary function of the IFCA would be the preservation of financial stability through the assumption of a *formal* role in negotiating the rescheduling of sovereign loans should borrowers encounter problems in servicing their debt. In order to be an effective neutral body, the IFCA would have to pool information on the creditworthiness of potential borrowers and on the sovereign loan exposures of the international banks. This need arises because of the nature of lending in the Euromarkets. Unlike the domestic banking system where a bank officer is able to assess creditworthiness based on direct knowledge of the potential borrower, only the final lender of Euromarket funds possesses knowledge of who the borrower is, as the average deposit passes through several banks before being passed on to the borrower. In addition, there is the unique nature of the sovereign loan: the lending bank cannot demand collateral nor can it take any action to safeguard itself against outright repudiation of the loan. Finally, the nature of Euromarket operations in the past has meant that banks increased their sovereign loan exposure without explicit knowledge of the activities of other lenders in the market.

Recently a number of international banks formed the Institute for International Finance (IIF), which has been given the task of pooling information on developing countries for member banks. Its formation reflects concern on the part of its members about the rising resource costs which have resulted from information problems of the sort described in the last paragraph. However, from the standpoint of international welfare this may not be the ideal solution to the problems. Radner and Stiglitz (1984) have proved the existence of a non-concavity in the net benefit from acquiring information. This means that when information is costly there are increasing returns to the pooling of information. Hence, a formal institution which made the information symmetric would be more efficient than piecemeal exchange of information by a small coalition of agents. It would also avoid the oligopolistic tendencies inherent in a body like the IIF, where the pooling of information is for a small group of private banks.

Some readers may worry that the proposal for an International Financial Co-ordination Agency would entail the proliferation of international bureaucracy. This need not be the case; human capital resources of the IMF and the World Bank could be diverted to this agency. The point is that neither of these institutions possesses the *formal* authority necessary for the successful operation of this new agency. For example, the main function of the IFCA is currently being assumed by the IMF, but its informal role could undermine confidence in the international banking system. International policy-makers must delegate the functions outlined earlier to some agency, and 'IFCA' is the most appropriate title for the body that assumes these responsibilities.

To summarize, the main duties of the IFCA would be:

(1) The assumption of a formal third-party role in the rescheduling process.
(2) The co-ordination of the lender of last resort function of the domestic central banks.
(3) Minimization of moral hazard and free rider problems.
(4) The pooling of information on trends in international lending, especially sovereign lending.

In this context, it is of interest to note the discussions at the IMF–World Bank meetings held in Seoul, South Korea, in October 1985. American delegates proposed the establishment of a semi-official body, which would assume the responsibility for the re-scheduling of developing country sovereign debt, and therefore, eliminate the current need for negotiation with a bank syndicate that can number more than 500 different banks. It was proposed that this organization should help in the co-ordination of the IMF and World Bank economic programmes. These suggestions go some way to meet the objectives of the IFCA, as discussed in preceding paragraphs.

Conclusion

This chapter began by examining the terms financial instability, financial crisis, insolvency and illiquidity as applied to the inter-national financial scene. It was argued that financial instability will be a consequence of a collapse of the international banking system. The real school interpretation of the causes of a financial crisis was discussed in terms of the international events responsible for creating severe debt-servicing difficulties for many sovereign borrowers. The situation was identified as one of crisis, which continues to threaten the stability of the international financial system. Various proposals put forward to deal with the crisis were reviewed. The optimal solution would be the formation of an International Financial Co-ordination Agency, which would deal with the unique aspects of sovereign borrowing. The goals of the IFCA are consistent with the banking school interpretation of the main role of a domestic central bank, although the means by which it would accomplish its objectives would be quite different. The IFCA would intervene directly should the need to reschedule arise, but it would not assume direct LLR responsibilities. These would be left to the national central banks, but the IFCA would act to eliminate any gaps that currently exist.

Notes: Chapter 5

1. See, among others, Fisher, 1932; Kindleberger, 1978a, 1978b; Minsky, 1977, 1982.
2. Official loans are rescheduled through the Paris Club. *The Economist* reports 64 Paris Club agreements since 1981 (see 'International monetary reform: a survey', *The Economist*, 5 October 1985, p. 26). As with commercial loan reschedulings, an IMF economic recovery programme has become an integral part of recent agreements.
3. This discussion of the new rules is drawn from the *Federal Reserve Bulletin*, February 1984, pp. 109–10.
4. For a full description of the banking and currency schools and their main proponents, see, among others, Andreades, 1966, 4th edn, part 1, chapters 4–6.
5. Nagatani, 1982, p. 11.

References

Andreades, A. (1966), *History of the Bank of England 1640–1903*, 4th edn (London: Frank, Cass & Company).

Angeloni, I. and Short, B. K. (1980), *The Impact of Country Risk Assessment on Eurocurrency Spreads: A Cross-Section Analysis*, Document DM/80/35 (Washington: International Monetary Fund).

Arrow, K. J. (1964), 'The role of securities in the optimal allocation of risk bearing', *Review of Economic Studies*, vol. 31, no. 2, pp. 91–6.

Bance, N. (1978), 'How our new money rating system works', *Euromoney*, October, p. 129.

Bareau, P. (1983), 'The lessons of an earlier international debt crisis', *The Banker*, December, pp. 35–9.

Batchelor, R. (1983), *The Avoidance of Catastrophe: Two 19th Century Banking Crises*, Monetary History Discussion Paper No. 10 (London: Centre for International Banking and Finance, The City University).

Batchelor, R. and Fitzgerald, D. (eds) (1986), *Financial Regulation* (London: Macmillan).

Beenstock, M. (1984), *The World Economy in Transition* (London: Allen & Unwin).

Beenstock, M. (1986), 'The theory of last resort lending', in Batchelor and Fitzgerald (eds), op. cit.

Bennett, P. (1984), 'Applying portfolio theory to global bank lending', *Journal of Banking and Finance*, vol. 8, pp. 153–69.

Burton, F. N. and Inoue, H. (1983), 'Country risk evaluation methods: a survey of systems in use', *The Banker*, January, pp. 41–3.

Cline, R. (1984), *International Debt: Systematic Risk and Policy Response* (Washington: Institute for International Economics; distributed by MIT Press).

Cooper, J. (1984), *The Management and Regulation of Banks* (London: Macmillan).

Debreu, G. (1959), *Theory of Value* (New York: Wiley).

Dennis, G. E. J. (1984), *International Financial Flows: A Statistical Handbook* (London: Graham & Trotman).

Dhonte, P. (1975), 'Describing external debt situations: roll over approach', *IMF Staff Papers*, no. 24, pp. 159–86.

Eaton, J. and Gersovitz, M. (1980), 'LDC participation in international financial markets', *Journal of Development Economics*, vol. 7, pp. 3–21.

Eaton, J. and Gersovitz, M. (1981a), *Poor Country Borrowing in Private Financial Markets and the Repudiation Issue*, Princeton Studies in International Finance No. 47 (Princeton, NJ: Princeton University Press).

Eaton, J. and Gersovitz, M. (1981b), 'Debt with potential repudiation: theoretical and empirical analysis', *Review of Economic Studies*, vol. 48, pp. 289–309.

Feder, G. and Just, R. (1977), 'A study of debt servicing capacity applying logit analysis', *Journal of Development Economics*, vol. 4, pp. 25–38.

Feder, G., Just, R. and Ross, K. (1981), 'Projecting debt servicing capacity of developing countries', *Journal of Financial and Quantitative Analysis*, vol. 16, no. 5, pp. 651–69.

Feder, G. and Ross, K. (1982), 'Risk assessments and risk premiums on the Eurodollar market', *Journal of Finance*, vol. 37, pp. 679–91.

Feldstein, M. S. (1969), 'Mean variance analysis in the theory of liquidity preference and portfolio selection', *Review of Economic Studies*, vol. 36, no. 1, pp. 5–12.

Fisher, I. (1932), *Booms and Depressions* (New York: Adelphi).

Fisk, C. and Rimlinger, F. (1979), 'Nonparametric estimates of LDC repayment prospects', *Journal of Finance*, vol. 34, pp. 429–35.

Frank, C. R., and Cline, R. (1971), 'Measurement of debt servicing capacity: an application of discriminant analysis', *Journal of International Economics*, vol. 1, pp. 327–44.

Friedman, I. S. (1984), *The World Debt Dilemma: Managing Country Risk* (Council for International Banking Studies, Washington, and Robert Morris Associates, Philadelphia).

Friedman, M. (1957), *A Theory of the Consumption Function* (Princeton, NJ: Princeton University Press).

Ghadar, F. (1982), 'Political risk and erosion of control', *Columbia Journal of World Business*, vol. 17, no. 3, pp. 47–51.

Goodman, S. H. (ed.) (1978), *Financing and Risk in Developing Countries* (London: Praeger Publishers).

Green, H. A. J. (1976), *Consumer Theory*, revised edn (London: Macmillan).

Guttenhag, J. and Herring, R. (1983), *The Lender of Last Resort Function in an International Context*, Princeton Essays in International Finance No. 151 (Princeton, NJ: Princeton University Press).

Hay, D. and Morris, D. (1979), *Industrial Economics* (Oxford: Oxford University Press).

Heenan, D. A., and Rummel, R. J. (1978), 'How multinationals analyse political risk', *Harvard Business Review*, January, pp. 67–76.

Heffernan, S. A. (1985), 'Country risk analysis: the demand and supply of sovereign loans', *Journal of International Money and Finance*, September, pp. 389–413.

Heffernan, S. A., Guerton, H. and Magee, A. (1983), 'Predicting sovereign debt rescheduling', *City University Business School Economic Review*, Autumn, pp. 25–32.

Heffernan, S. A., Delmain, M., and Hollist, B. (1985a), 'Measuring the performance of rescheduled sovereign loans', *City University Business School Economic Review*, Spring, pp. 36–9.

Heffernan, S. A., Delmain, M., and Hollist, B. (1985b), 'How international banks analyse country risk', mimeo (London: City University Business School).

Herring, R. J. (ed.) (1983), *Managing International Risk* (London: Cambridge University Press).

Hirshleifer, J. (1965), 'Investment decisions under uncertainty: choice theoretic approaches', *Quarterly Journal of Economics*, vol. 79, no. 4, pp. 509–36.

IMF (1983), *World Economic Outlook*, Occasional Paper No. 21 (Washington: International Monetary Fund).

IMF (1984), *World Economic Outlook*, Occasional Paper No. 27 (Washington: International Monetary Fund).

IMF (1985), *International Financial Statistics* (Washington: International Monetary Fund).

Jenks, L. H. (1927), *The Migration of British Capital to 1875* (London: Alfred A. Knopf).

Johnson, R. B. (1983), *The Economics of the Euro-Market* (London: Macmillan).

Kharas, H. (1984), 'The long run creditworthiness of developing countries: theory and practice', *Quarterly Journal of Economics*, vol. XCIX, no. 3, pp. 415–39.

Kindleberger, C. P. (1978a), 'Debt situation of developing countries in historical perspective', in S. H. Goodman (ed.), op. cit.

Kindleberger, C. P. (1978b), *Manias, Panics and Crashes: A History of Financial Crises* (New York: Basic Books).

Kindleberger, C. P. and Laffargue, J. P. (eds) (1982), *Financial Crises: Theory, History and Policy* (New York: Cambridge University Press).

Kletzer, K. M. (1984), 'Asymmetries of information and LDC borrowing with sovereign risk', *Economic Journal*, vol. 94, pp. 287–307.

Lewis, W. A. (1978), *Growth and Fluctuations, 1870–1913* (London: Allen & Unwin).

Markowitz, H. M. (1959), *Portfolio Selection* (New York: Wiley).

Mathis, F. J. and Maslin, D. C. (1981), 'The RMA survey of the management of international loan portfolio diversification', *Journal of Commercial Bank Lending*, March, pp. 36–44.

Mayo, A. L. and Barrett, A. G. (1978), 'An early warning model for assessing country risk' in S. H. Goodman (ed.), op. cit, pp. 81–7.

Minsky, H. P. (1977), 'A theory of systematic fragility', in E. J. Altman and A. W. Sametz (eds), *Financial Crises: Institutions and Markets in a Fragile Environment* (New York: Wiley), pp. 138–52.

Minsky, H. P. (1982), 'The financial instability hypothesis: capitalist processes and the behaviour of the world economy' in Kindleberger and Laffargue (eds), op. cit, pp. 13–46.

Modigliani, F. and Miller, M. H. (1958), 'The cost of capital, corporation finance and the theory of investment', *American Economic Review*, vol. 48, no. 3, pp. 261–97.

Nagatani, K. (1982), *What Central Banks Really Are*, Discussion Paper No. 82–07 (Vancouver: Department of Economics, University of British Columbia).

Radner, R. and Stiglitz, J. (1984), 'A non-concavity in the value of information', in M. Boyer and R. E. Kilstrom (eds), *Bayesian Models in Economic Theory* (Amsterdam: North Holland), pp. 33–52.

Sachs, J. and Kyle, S. (1985), *Developing Country Debt and the Market Value of Large Commercial Banks*, NBER Working Paper No. 1470 (Washington: National Bureau of Economic Research).

Saini, K. and Bates, P. (1984), 'A survey of the quantitative approaches to country risk analysis', *Journal of Banking and Finance*, no. 8, pp. 341–56.

Santomero, A. M. (1984), 'Modeling the banking firm, a survey', *Journal of Money, Credit and Banking*, vol. 16, no. 4 (November, part 2), pp. 576–602.

Shapiro, A. C. (1982), *Multinational Financial Management* (New York: Allyn and Bacon).

Southard, F. A. (1979), *The Evolution of the International Monetary Fund*, Princeton Essays in International Finance No. 135 (Princeton, NJ: Princeton University Press).

Suttle, P. (1985), 'Debt projection models: a survey and comparison', mimeo (London: Bank of England).

Taffler, R. and Abassi, B. (1982), *Country Risk: A Model of Economic Performance Related to Debt Servicing Capacity*, City University Business School Working Paper No. 36 (London: The City University).

Taffler, R. and Abassi, B. (1984), 'Country risk: a model of economic performance related to debt servicing capacity', *Journal of the Royal Statistical Society*, series A, part 4, pp. 541–68.

Walter, I. (1981), 'Country risk, portfolio decisions and regulation in international bank lending', *Journal of Banking and Finance*, vol. 5, pp. 77–92 (special issue).

Watchel, P. (ed.) (1982), *Crises in the Economic and Financial Structure* (New York: Lexington Books).

World Bank (1984–5), *World Debt Tables* (Washington: The World Bank).

World Bank (1984), *World Development Report 1984* (Oxford: Oxford University Press).

World Bank (1985), *World Development Report 1985* (Oxford: Oxford University Press).

Further Reading

American Express International Banking Corporation (1982), 'Private bank lending to developing countries' and 'Sovereign debt rescheduling: implications for private banks', *The AMEX Bank Review* Special Papers No. 3 and No. 4, July.

American Express International Banking Corporation (1984), 'International debt, banks and the LDCs', *The AMEX Bank Review* Special Papers No. 10, March.

Avramovic, D. and Gulhati, R. (1958), *Debt Servicing Capacity and Post War Growth in International Indebtedness* (Baltimore: Johns Hopkins Press).

Avramovic, D. et al. (1964), *Economic Growth and External Debt* (Baltimore: Johns Hopkins Press).

Bank of England (1985), 'The international banking and capital markets in 1984', *Bank of England Quarterly Bulletin*, March, pp. 58–68.

Bernanke, B. S. (1983), 'Nonmonetary effects of the financial crisis in the propagation of the Great Depression', *American Economic Review*, vol. 73, pp. 257–76.

Brau, E. *et al.* (1983), *Recent Multilateral Debt Reschedulings and Bank Creditors*, IMF Occasional Paper No. 25 (Washington: International Monetary Fund).

Cairncross, A. K. (1953), *Home and Foreign Investment 1870–1913* (Cambridge: Cambridge University Press).

Carron, A. S. (1982), *Financial Crises: Recent Experiences in US and International Markets*, Brookings Papers on Economic Activity No. 2, pp. 395–418.

Collyns, C. (1983), *Alternatives to the Central Bank in the Developing World*, IMF Occasional Paper No. 20 (Washington: International Monetary Fund).

Crockett, A. (1977), *International Money: Issues and Analysis* (London: Nelson).

Ford, A. G. (1962), *The Gold Standard, 1880–1914* (Oxford: Oxford University Press).

Goldstein, E. and Vanous, J. (1983), 'Country risk analysis: pitfalls of comparing Eastern Bloc countries with the rest of the World', *Columbia Journal of World Business*, vol. 18, no. 4, pp. 10–16.

Goodman, L. S. *et al.* (1982), 'Risks and international bank lending: a panel discussion', in P. Watchel (ed.) *Crises in the Economic and Financial Structure* (New York: Lexington Books), pp. 257–71.

Guttenhag, J. and Herring, R. (1982), 'The insolvency of financial institutions: assessment and regulatory disposition', in P. Watchel (ed.) *Crises in the Economic and Financial Structure* (New York: Lexington Books), pp. 99–126.

Heffernan, S. A. (1985), 'Reflections on the case for an international central bank', *Greek Economic Review*, April, pp. 99–120.

Heffernan, S. A. (1986), 'The costs and benefits of international banking', in R. Batchelor and D. Fitzgerald (eds), *Financial Regulation* (London: Macmillan).

Kindleberger, C. P. (1984), *A Financial History of Western Europe* (London: Allen & Unwin).

McDonald, D. (1982), 'Debt capacity and developing country borrowing: a survey of the literature', *IMF Staff Papers*, August, pp. 603–46.

Mathis, F. J. (ed.) (1975), *Offshore Lending by US Commercial Banks* (Washington: Bankers' Association for Foreign Trade).

Nagy, P. (1984), *Country Risk* (London: Euromoney Publications).

Press, S. J. and Wilson, S. (1978), 'Choosing between logit regression and discriminant analysis', *Journal of the American Statistical Society*, vol. 73, pp. 699–705.

Reid, M. (1982), *The Secondary Banking Crisis, 1973–75* (London: Macmillan).

Sachs, J. (1982), 'LDC debt in the 1980s: risk and reform', in P. Watchel (ed.), *Crises in the Economic and Financial Structure* (New York: Lexington Books).

Sachs, J. (1985), *Theoretical Issues in International Borrowing*, Princeton Studies in International Finance No. 54 (Princeton, NJ: Princeton University Press).

Sachs, J. and Cohen, D. (1982), *LDC Borrowing with Default Risk*, NBER Working Paper No. 925 (Washington: National Bureau of Economic Research).

Solow, R. (1982), 'On the lender of last resort', in C. P. Kindleberger and J. P. Laffargue (eds.), *Financial Crises: Theory, History and Policy* (New York: Cambridge University Press), pp. 237–55.

Williamson, J. (1983), 'Keynes and the international economic order', in D. Worsick and J. Trevithick (eds.), *Keynes and the Modern World* (Cambridge: Cambridge University Press), pp. 87–127.

Index